SHUT UP, GET LEAN

PRAISE FOR
SHUT UP, GET LEAN

"Through his transparency, communication and ability to get others all moving in the same direction, Ray Leathers has displayed some of the strongest leadership skills I have encountered. He combines those skills with his love for Lean practices, and this book is the result. Many leaders from many sectors would benefit from reading *Shut Up, Get Lean*."

Jennifer Mackin

CEO, Oliver Group, Inc., a leadership development firm

"With straight talk and pithy examples, Leathers illuminates how a leader in any organization can engage in clear thinking and solid execution to achieve bold goals. Ray makes a concise case that leaders fully control the necessary ingredients to train for deep cultural change — talent, tools and time. His penetrating analysis of the reality of leading systemic change, coupled with his concise advice to leaders, captures the emotions, mindsets and methods possessed by leaders who produce great results. If you are action-oriented and believe that changing anything requires not just a new way of *thinking*, but also a new way of *doing*, then this book is for you."

James Neihof

Superintendent, Shelby County Public Schools

"What Ray accomplishes with *Shut Up, Get Lean* is to combine and describe concisely fundamental insights derived from an upbringing in rural Kentucky, a distinctive military career in the US army, detailed knowledge of Japanese management techniques, and comprehensive knowledge of the inner dynamics of a large multinational European based manufacturing group. And he applied all this knowledge to managing a Kentucky-based manufacturing company, where he was supported by distinguished CI experts like Susan Nally. It made the company quadruple its revenue during his tenure and highly successful on the earnings side. What else can I say?"

Günther Felderer
Member of the Board, voestalpine Metal Forming GmbH

"In *Shut Up, Get Lean*, Ray Leathers deftly blends his experiences — growing up in Kentucky, serving in the military and working in various manufacturing roles — to share true thought leadership about the importance of culture and continuous improvement for driving success in today's marketplace. No matter your industry, his practical and thoughtful ideas can be put to work immediately to help fuel higher levels of performance. A must-read for leaders trying to navigate in an ever-changing world!"

David M. Bowling
CEO, Citizens Union Bank

"Ray continues to be an inspiration, and now he is doing it in written form through the completion of this new book! The book effectively illustrates the fundamentals of Lean and continuous improvement, plus highlights the critical aspects of culture, all woven together by a proven strong leader with a track record of success."

Derek Ludwig

Global Vice President, Procurement, Steelcase Inc.

"I thoroughly enjoyed this book. Straight talk and straight from the heart. Written by a leader who has been there and done it! Ray and Susan amplify the significance of a strong culture thriving on continuous improvement and inspiring the entire team to drive improvement. *Shut Up, Get Lean* is peppered with tidbits of wisdom, encouragement, guidance and the humble recognition of life's many blessings. Read it, pass it on and get to it!"

Mike Carroll

President/CEO, Steel Technologies

"I've known Ray for nearly 20 years and this book (just like Ray) is clear, concise and straight to the point. Most leadership books talk in circles and are filled with the latest buzzwords that leave you wondering what the authors are really trying to say. But not *Shut Up, Get Lean*; it cuts to the chase and provides straightforward directions on how to be more effective, reduce costs and improve efficiency."

Steven Y. Summers

PE Executive Vice President, Gray Construction

"Determining the best approach to achieving business improvement objectives is always challenging. Ray and Susan have developed and shared a proven process for establishing a positive culture of engagement that delivers real impact to businesses. This book provides a practical guide to achieving improved moral AND financial reward for the business and the associates who participate."

Michael Hesketh
President and Owner, Superb IPC

"I have personally witnessed Ray Leathers and his team transform a stalled organization into a highly productive culture passionately committed to excellence. In this must-read book, Ray has distilled his 40 years of experience, lessons-learned and accumulated best practices (from CI experts like Susan Nally!) into a simple, but effective, handbook with immediately applicable tools and practices. The Leathers leadership style blends courage and commitment to build a culture that fully embraces the tools and methods of continuous improvement."

Doug Semenick
CSP, Semenick & Assoc., Inc., a leadership training company

"Successful business leaders are acutely aware of the importance of culture and the ability to leverage the dynamics it provides to drive and build a business. It's critical that the business culture embrace the concept of continuous improvement to allow the business to evolve. Accordingly, Ray and Susan's book is a must-read for anyone who harbors the desire to optimize the success of their business by leveraging culture. Ray and Sue have provided simple common-sense concepts and tools that can be used by any organization dependent on the effectiveness of its most important resource: people."

Steve Meador
President, Pegasus Solutions Group,
2017 Kentucky's Manufacturer of the Year

"I enjoyed 17 years working with Ray, learning from him, and seeing firsthand how his CIP roadmap can transform an organization. In *Shut Up, Get Lean*, he and Susan provide the proven methodology for creating the right culture and tools needed for Lean operations. Ray has the courage to recognize that even the CI process requires improvement on a regular basis, and that leadership has responsibility to actively engage and promote CI because 'people watch what the boss watches.'"

Kevin Dierking
President/CEO, voestalpine Roll Forming Corporation

Shut Up, Get Lean

How to Stop
Simply Talking About
Lean Manufacturing
and Actually Start
Building Your
Culture of
Continuous
Improvement

RAY LEATHERS and SUSAN A. NALLY

SILVER TREE
PUBLISHING

Shut Up, Get Lean: How to Stop Simply Talking About Lean Manufacturing and Actually Start Building Your Culture of Continuous Improvement

Copyright 2019 by Ray Leathers and Susan A. Nally

Published by Silver Tree Publishing, a division of Silver Tree Communications, LLC (Kenosha, WI). www.SilverTreeCommunications.com

Editing by:
Kate Colbert

Cover design and typesetting by:
Courtney Hudson

Proofreading by:
Jessica Gardner

First edition, March 2019

ISBN: 978-1-948238-09-0

Library of Congress Control Number: 2018960182

Created in the United States of America

"The purpose of life is not to be happy. It is to be useful, to be honorable, to be compassionate, to have it make some difference that you have lived and lived well."

— *Ralph Waldo Emerson*

Dedication

To the humble, industrious workers who naturally honed these tools to perfection without knowing the tools had names and who never asked to be recognized for using them.

And for the servant-hearted leaders who believe everyone performing work *deserves* a stable and repeatable process.

Table of Contents

Foreword

Corporate culture is the basis for everything that is being done in organizations. Unfortunately, the importance of culture is often seriously underestimated. It is easy to fall back into old habits, to fire-fight on daily operations and to simply neglect nurturing the organizational culture. Corporate culture is about more than just creating identity, it is the intentional defining and authentic living of values. It is deeply rooted in a company's vision, strategy and organizational structure. It defines how we approach our employees, our customers, investors and the greater public.

A healthy corporate culture has an enormous leverage. It should never be underestimated.

So why am I talking about corporate culture in the foreword of a book on Lean Management? Well, as I've already said — and this cannot be stressed enough — culture is the basis for everything. The success of Lean implementation relies very much on corporate culture.

Ask yourself these questions:

- How can processes be improved if they are not being understood?

- How can those new processes be maintained and successful if people do not understand why certain things are being done in certain ways?

- How can people avoid mistakes if they do not collaborate with each other?

- How can people be inspired if they are not actively involved?

- How can companies thrive if their people are not empowered to make their own decisions, and if they are not supported by their managers?

The best Lean principles will only be effective and work if they are aligned with the existing or desired cultural infrastructure. It is therefore vital to go beyond simply defining Lean Management tools to be implemented, and to actually nurture the corporate culture. If there is a missing link or even a conflict created between the organizational culture and defined Lean processes, neither of the two will work out, let alone be effective or successful. Culture is key to turn the changes required by Lean Management into practice.

What I have learned in my role as a top manager for more than two decades is that empowering people is one key success factor. Only when you increase accountability can an organization move forward. And increasing accountability means encouraging people to make decisions (including risks) and allowing them to fail from time to time. The people are the heart of an organization. If they are motivated and have an actual role to play in that process of getting Lean and improving, acceptance is high and success comes naturally.

Employees absolutely need to be empowered and supported to both identify problems and find solutions in order to achieve better results. *The basis or bedrock for this to work is trust.* An organization without trust simply doesn't work. If you are a manager, you are frequently confronted with a kind of dressed-up truth, because employees are afraid of confronting their bosses with the uncompromising truth of facts. And this is what needs to change.

How to get there? It takes time and has to be lived from the top. Leaders must walk that talk. Otherwise, you are neither authentic nor credible. Simply put: It requires a change of culture for most organizations, especially big corporations.

Continuous improvement relies on a healthy corporate culture. What is the ultimate goal of efforts taken into the direction of Lean Management? *Excellence.* At the end of the day, it is all about maximizing customer value through perfect performance and results.

Ray Leathers, who I have known for many years, has boiled it down to the essentials in this book. It is never about talking — about creating fancy posters or giveaways — but it is about walking that talk. Through his use of metaphors and analogies, combined with practical lessons and anecdotes from his military service, Ray makes this book easy to read.

If you want to climb that mountain all the way to the summit of Lean excellence, Ray Leathers and his co-author Susan A. Nally provide you with the perfect map to that destination. *Read this book, then get ready to do the work.* The stamina and actual walking has to be done by you, and you can do it. Ray underlines this importance of accountability, and draws attention to the fact that errors are opportunities. Ray, a military man with excellent business sense, served voestalpine for almost two decades. During his time with us, he created an outstanding continuous improvement culture. This has not only been recognized by us at voestalpine, but throughout the industry, where Ray is regarded as a leading expert in continuous improvement culture.

Ray has always represented the future, and the spirit he has spread within voestalpine remains unforgotten. I am honored and feel privileged to write this foreword for my dear friend, business partner and colleague, who I think of very highly. I recommend that everyone who is interested in moving organizations forward read this book. Ray understands that continuous improvement is a philosophy and a permanent decision. It should not be viewed as a project; there is no defined end and you are never finished with improving.

The biggest room in the world is the room for improvement.

Peter Schwab
Head of the Metal Forming Division and
Member of the Board of voestalpine AG

PROLOGUE: A MESSAGE FROM RAY

Leaders, take note: Your culture is already determining the cadence and syncopation of all the proverbial music you will write for your businesses and for your people. If you are ready to create something new, it's vital that you create something worth protecting and worthy of emulation. It is my hope that this book gives you some inspiration and tools to do just that.

In writing this book, it was important to me that its lessons reflected many voices — not just a view from the C-suite but also the practical truths as articulated by continuous improvement Lean Manufacturing specialists and those who work daily in service and industry fields. So, I consulted with colleagues and trusted advisors — most especially my co-author Susan A. Nally — whose vantage points, when added to mine, provide what I believe to be a broad, clear view of what works, what matters and what the future holds.

Throughout *Shut Up, Get Lean*, you'll be invited to view your work — and the entire ecosystems of organizations and cultures — from fresh perspectives. I will offer you mine — the viewpoint and recommendations of a veteran president of a $125 million company employing more than 400 employees. And I'll offer those opinions of my colleagues and advisors as well — up, down and across the organization, where people have stopped simply talking about Lean Manufacturing and actually started building remarkable cultures of continuous improvement.

In this book, I have endeavored to explore just a few, vital topics for you, the reader:

- Values
- Culture setting
- Straight talk on what I've seen, experienced and learned

A President's Perspective

- Efficiency systems
- Simplification of Lean tools
- Success strategies

Distilled and simplified for your rapid application

This book is perhaps best enjoyed if the opening chapters and stories are read sequentially, though I have designed this book to be a resource guide that allows you to jump straight to the Lean Tools or other sections that you most urgently want to explore. Go ahead — jump ahead. Use the Table of Contents to guide your strategy to putting *Shut Up, Get Lean* to work for you.

To help you, the reader, to have some perspective of the journey, let us tell you a little about the company where we created most of the experiences you will encounter in the subsequent pages of this book. voestalpine Roll Forming Corporation (RFC) produces metal structural components utilizing the roll forming process, and supplying multiple industries (e.g., aerospace, automotive, office furniture and seating, agricultural equipment and distribution systems). Roll forming is the most economical production process for the continuous bending of metal channels, angles and complex shapes with multiple bends. It is a cold-forming process that gradually bends (blooms) flat metal into a finished, uniform profile by passing it through a series of progressive mated tool dies.

voestalpine Roll Forming Corporation, a wholly owned subsidiary of voestapline (VA), is a complete profit center to include sales and marketing, product development, research and development, tool design and build, and manufacturing. voestalpine Roll Forming Corporation company has six plants in three states (Kentucky, Indiana and Pennsylvania) with sister companies on nearly every continent. RFC was started by a private individual in 1947 and has been at its current location since 1963. It was acquired by voestalpine AG in 2000, the year I joined as vice president of operations. RFC currently employees more than 450 team members and has grown to more than $150 million in sales. After the acquisition, voestalpine management provided the autonomy necessary for our team to create the continuous improvement culture it enjoys today and capital for its successful growth. The importance of these two dynamics cannot be over emphasized! Too many times, business owners or corporate executive staffs seek to impose "cookie-cutter" policies and procedures that ultimately restrict local creativity and ownership to drive culture change. Another book could be written to address these challenges and opportunities. Let this be sufficient to illustrate, to those owners and corporate staffs that may read this book, the importance of these two factors, *autonomy and capital,* are a testament to the voestalpine AG values that drove both growth and success, evidenced in the process we present here.

SECTION 1

SHUTTING UP

Listening to the Lessons that Can Transform Your Business

Chapter 1
Open Season

You're reading this because you are in *a season of change.* Metaphorically, you're hunting and your timing is perfect — it's open season! Let me begin with encouragement. Take courage, sustainable change is not easy for anyone; it is a demanding personal mission. It could destroy you. However, if you refuse to embrace change, you're already extinct.

Open season is an exciting and rare season that many leaders miss. It is good to be you. Open season is a time to reap the harvest you have been sowing and planting your entire career. Choosing change is to reap and begin anew.

> **Open season is a time to reap the harvest you have been sowing and planting your entire career.**

- Are you tired?

- Frustrated?

- Feel like the weekend is the only time you ever have any real accomplishment?

- Does leveraging your personal inspiration and creativity feel like working a rusted saw through an ash limb?

If so, you may be ripe for change.

- Has it been a long time since you easily commanded change?

- Are you secretly troubled, fearful that what appeared to be your influence in past outcomes may have been simply circumstance or timing?

- Do you wonder, *have I, can I, make any difference anymore* — especially as it relates to outcomes involving the people who matter the most to you?

- Does the weight of the needed change feel too heavy, impossible?

Don't ignore these signs; open season is almost here.

Choosing change is change ... it is *new* thinking. Thinking new thoughts about old problems is particularly hard when years of inertia have rusted over the truth of the situation, stalled your intuition and stolen your hope. If the flagstones of your personal success have been replaced with frustration, impatience, cynicism and/or hopelessness, and if you recognize that in yourself or your organization, change is already at work in your spirit, be encouraged. You recognized it. That is a victory.

> Thinking new thoughts about old problems is particularly hard when years of inertia have rusted over the truth of the situation, stalled your intuition and stolen your hope.

Looking in the rearview mirror, across more than 40 years, I have anticipated open season each year — literally and figuratively. Since childhood, there has been no greater sporting pleasure for me than hunting game across the bluegrass fields and streams of Kentucky. In service, as CEO of a large Kentucky company, I have enjoyed equal enthusiasms and have rewarded the "hunting" of business ventures in corporate boardrooms and manufacturing fields. It is my experience that three things make a hunter in the field or on Wall Street successful: *preparation, skill and the will to change or adapt.*

Change requires a catalyst; both positive and negative stimulus moves us to action, to change. We all know from our human experience that negative stimulus moves us faster than positive stimulus. If you burn the frog, he will jump; if you gently heat and then boil him, he will not wake up from the steam bath. When you acknowledge your suffering or pain that awareness is a gift, unwrap it. Whatever suffering pressed you to pick up this book; blessing or curse, it has been a catalyst in your thinking, and I urge you to use it as such.

This is your open season; something new is about to begin. It would be a travesty to sleep through the first day of open season, I know from personal experience. You are bound to miss the best opportunities and they may never return.

This book is a field map and a coaching guide. My intent is to help you prepare for the storm. Preparation and skill are the critical first steps toward embracing change. It is my belief that you can sustain a successful culture of continuous improvement with these tools. Your season is open.

Chapter 2
Know Thyself - Effective Leadership

A brief working definition of an effective leader:

> *Effective leaders are passionate, charismatic people, who are physically compelled to take action, who naturally attract others to take equal or greater action. They are prepared, skilled and unafraid of change. Leaders get people to willingly do what needs to be done.*

Are you a leader? Are you effective? There is a big difference between these two questions. And it's a difference that most leaders don't consider until it's too late. Your honest answer about your effectiveness is critically important. We have all been led. We had had the sense of sitting "under leaders," and many of us have suffered under weak leaders. But we all aspire to work *alongside* an effective leader. We rise to the level of talent we partner with ... show me your colleagues and I will show you your future.

> We rise to the level of talent we partner with ... show me your colleagues and I will show you your future.

When you are on the sidelines, and not in the action, do you feel anxious, competitive, and/or resentful that you can't jump in and make it (whatever "it" is) happen? If the answer is *yes*, you're a leader and probably a control freak too. Welcome to my world. That is okay, as long as you are a self-aware control freak and understand that real leadership means you are actually leading people, not pushing or enabling others.

So what about being effective? How can you evaluate your personal effectiveness? Look to the fruit (or lack of fruit) developing from the people entrusted to you. Personal effectiveness is directly correlated to a leader's ability to move those entrusted to a desired result or effect. If you're helping others to succeed, you too are successful.

You're not alone if you can't name the secret ingredient that moves people to action, and if you find yourself stuck, sinking in bottomless quick sand. All the 360-degree evaluations in the world won't set you free from the private fear that your own leadership paradigm may be incorrect.

If one more person offers you a change seminar or coaching blog, or leaves a teambuilding book on your desk, you're going to pound someone like they were a fifth-grade bully stealing your sister's lunch money.

If you are still with me, still reading … you're ready. It is my prayer you learn from my pain, my experience, my failures and my success. May this work provide deeper insight and tangible tools in the effective implementation of change in your life.

Dan Millman, in his book *Way of the Peaceful Warrior*, suggested that, "The secret of change is to focus all of your energy, not on fighting the old, but on building the new." Indeed. It is time to build the new.

IMPLEMENTING REAL CHANGE

Probably you are in charge or leading something: it might be a sports team, a church group or a large company. Whatever you're shepherding, it needs help ... improvement. Whether you need to boost sales (and profits), increase your customer base and employee satisfaction, or just defend yourself from the threats of competition, you're holding a book that describes good old horse-sense tools that cut away waste and offers strategies that increase your personal ability to impact cultural success within any organization.

This is a story about implementing *real* change. More than change, this material intends to be a strategic allegory that tunes the reader's ear to keenly identify waste within a system and call *bulls#!+* on the time-honored, energy-wasting activities that deafen the quarterback positions on your team.

Shut Up, Get Lean is your roadmap, hand-drawn on the back of a picnic napkin, detailing how a traditional manufacturing culture evolved into an energized, empowered employee-driven Lean culture. This work is meant to help young leaders get in front of this invisible thing called "culture" and leverage it to empower your greatest, most valued resource: *people.* This work will encourage you to habitually and unashamedly invest personally and passionately in your people. You must become their greatest cheerleader, the fan who makes all the other players secretly wish you had come to see *them* play. Throw your beer in the air when team members break down walls and score Hail Mary miracle plays for your organization. A paramount precept of this material is to inspire you, the leader, personally; it's about building a living, breathing culture that is self-inspiring, self-challenging and self-improving.

> A paramount precept of this material is to inspire
> you, the leader, personally; it's about building
> a living, breathing culture that is self-inspiring,
> self-challenging and self-improving.

Several years ago, the manufacturing operation I was running was acquired by owners who demanded improvement — or else. I loved my organization, but it was handicapped by outdated technology, under-qualified and under-motivated staff, and a management team ill-prepared to lead this new charge. The stakes were high, the climb was steep and the team was already weary.

My immediate challenge was to get this organization to align with engaged leadership, and to do it quickly! When you are at the top of an organization, regardless of its altitude or importance, ultimately your success is dependent on the response of your peer team to your leadership. You are propelled or de-railed by the folks who work directly with you and beside you. They are the most honest reflection of your leadership. Absolute alignment among peer leaders is a critical first step in being an effective leader. *Note*: Not absolute agreement, but alignment. And it is worth repeating: there is no alignment without bedrock trust.

> "You see, we are like blocks of stone out of which
> the sculptor carves forms of men. The blows of HIS
> chisel, which hurt so much, are what make us perfect.
> God wants us to love, to be loved and to grow up."
>
> — *C.S. Lewis*

I had to prepare my young staff for exponential growth, speed-of-light technology digitization, engineering trials, market volatility and a tidal wave of new human talent. Change was necessary for our very survival. Over the years, we would need to hone our culture and Lean tools, cutting away the chaff and focusing on the identification of methodologies that deliver sustainable results.

The organization I was honored to shepherd has grown into one of the top-producing subsidiaries of a global corporate entity. Today, it is a company in the top 5 percent of profitability in its sector. If I am prone to stumble over pride, it is pride in the generation of leaders that I was privileged to serve and help advance.

In two words, we called our philosophy, our structure, our mindset and our daily culture ... *continuous improvement.*

A NEW WAY OF APPROACHING CONTINUOUS IMPROVEMENT

If you research the term "continuous improvement" (CI, as I will often abbreviate it in this book), you will step into an infinite list of materials and opinions on the subject. The concept, now a modern-day buzz phrase, connects itself invasively to many other efficiency topics: cultural engineering, team building, cost reducing, kaizen, ROI, Toyota Lean Manufacturing and more. Continuous Improvement is an umbrella term, covering many academic perspectives on how a person leverages culture. It seems that there are as many forms and applications of continuous improvement as there are stars in the sky.

The term "continuous improvement" means different things to different people. One might think of any number of English and Japanese pioneers, like Ford, Deming, Covey, Taylor, Drucker, Ohno, Shingo, as well as their manufactured buzzwords *kaizen, Plan-Do-Check-Act (PDCA), Value Stream Mapping, Lean Methodology or just-in-time,* introduced to the manufacturing executive's vocabulary. My advice is to expose yourself to as much continuous improvement discussion as possible so that you'll be able to leverage successful concepts and ultimately design a contiguous Continuous Improvement Culture for yourself.

Obviously, there are no new or original concepts here. There is nothing new under the sun; everything in this text was unashamedly borrowed.

What is different about this work is that it represents the best cherry-picked ideas, cooked down into an efficiency jam recipe, which has proven successful. You'll see references to the work of others; you'll also hear about the practices I've used and how they worked in my case. As I did before you, keep yourself reading, ask questions and study the best of the best cherry-pickers, knowing that their recipes are rarely published. At the end of this book, you will find a list of books my colleagues and I have found extremely helpful for ideation in continuous improvement concepts.

A word of caution ... continuous improvement is a permanent decision to engage in culture, meaning you will have to resource it and support it fully. It's not a seminar or weekend workshop where, when you get to some destination, you're done. You never stop improving — that's the point. And it's a reflexive ideology: it applies to itself. You have to improve the continuous improvement system as well. To feed that monster, you have to commit yourself to certain habits, among them a commitment of time and thought, a willingness to accept criticisms and failures, and a drive to keep learning.

> **A word of caution ... continuous improvement is a permanent decision to engage in culture, meaning you will have to resource it and support it fully.**

Right now, your competition is training; SHUT UP AND TRAIN.

A 'truism' I learned along the way? Training is the most important thing we do; it is also the *worst* thing we do. The only organization that I was part of that perfected training was the U.S. Army. Our military personnel only do two things: fight and train. In the military, if training is not effective, you die. That is a lot of motivation! We constantly profess how important we believe skills, teamwork and leadership training is to the success of our operations. Yet, we quickly sacrifice our serious Monday morning training convictions to meet Friday afternoon's late shipment. This habit of neglecting training is deadly. This trade-off is paramount to erecting a building without a foundation. Although functional, it will not survive the first storm or have a productive life.

Would you turn your child loose to drive your car without some form of driver's education and demonstrated experience? Doubtful. Yet, we do this every day in manufacturing. We send new employees to the production floor without proper training on processes and equipment. Worse, we elevate promising team members to management and leadership positions without any inclination of ability or basic training in the essential skills for oversight of subordinates. Then we sit back and attempt to analyze and solve labor and efficiency challenges. *Creating a culture of continuous improvement will require an investment in training.*

Many leaders make the mistake of attempting to implement a CI Culture by jumping straight to training Lean skills, i.e., problem solving, kaizens, kanbans, etc. Let me be clear on this point — an organization's leadership must commit to the process first by creating a system, a road map, a foundation that will dictate the training required to sustain the CI Culture. This includes determining the values the team will embrace, and creating experiences to reinforce the values, which in turn drives behaviors that produce actions and results. To paraphrase the famous saying from the 1989 film *Field of Dreams*, "Build it and they will come."

A RECIPE FOR CI SUCCESS

There are just three ingredients in the recipe for a culture of continuous improvement: *values, culture and tools.* Everything, we will explore in the pages of this book falls into one of these three categories. Unlike many other company leaders or even CI authorities, I place significant worth on the importance of *culture construction* and will emphasize it accordingly. The tools associated with effective leadership can be practical, useful, even genius, but they are lifeless without human touch, and we would all do well to remember that.

> The tools associated with effective leadership can be practical, useful, even genius, but they are lifeless without human touch, and we would all do well to remember that.

By way of example, I encourage you to think about your living situation as an analogy for your workplace. There is the house where you *physically live* (a tool) and then there is this invisible, but very tangible, idea of *what you protect in the house* (your values), and all of this is seen by *how you live* (your culture) with others in that house. This is such a simple concept, but it's all too common for people and organizations to miss the importance of these ingredients, and to pay little heed to how they are mixed into the organizational recipe. Use this analogy to remind yourself why it's important to (1) identify a system for creating a values-driven culture and (2) quickly identify the most powerful tools that reinforce and protect the people "living" in your organizational house for generations to come.

Continuous improvement is a lifelong journey, and it will take scary twists, force you to try out some new ideas and risk a lot of yourself along the way. But if you tackle the job of building a continuous improvement culture revolution with integrity and hope, it will be the most rewarding work you ever do in life.

"We can't solve problems by using the same kind of thinking we used when we created them."

— *Albert Einstein*

Chapter 3
THE IMPORTANCE OF CULTURE

What is more important — an organizational strategy or organizational culture?

Any company failing to connect the two — strategy and culture — is putting its success at risk. Many studies show there is a direct correlation between a healthy, productive culture and a company's bottom line. Yet, the majority of companies spend little time thinking about (let alone *doing* anything about) this topic ... even when they're spending lots of time thinking about their business strategy.

> **"Culture eats strategy for breakfast."**
>
> — *Peter Drucker*

There is a powerful trinity that must be considered before change transformations can effectively take place — the intersection of strategy, capability and culture. All three need to be designed together, aligned and enabling each other to create true organizational transformation.

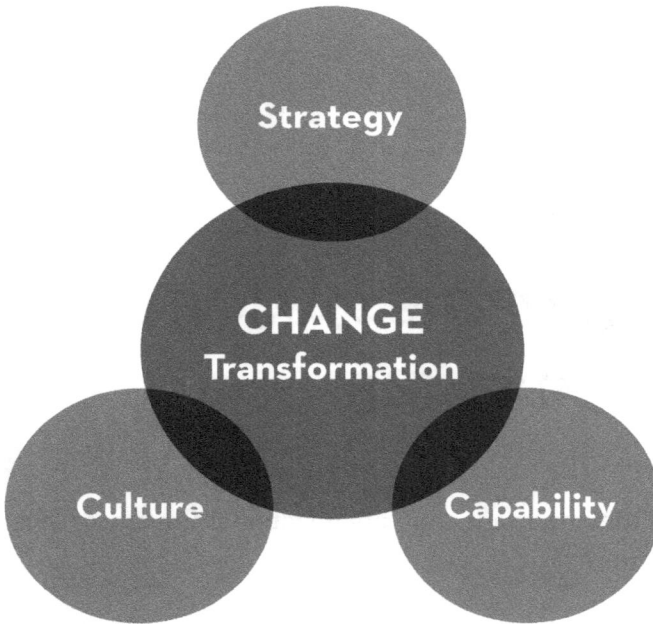

Corporate culture is a difficult thing to master. In many ways, it can be a moving target. Culture might mean something different to everyone in your organization. Regardless of your effort to cultivate culture (even if you ignore it altogether), your culture exists, it grows and it continues to evolve with the passage of time. It is the result of action and reaction. It is the lingering effect of every human interaction.

> Regardless of your effort to cultivate culture (even if you ignore it altogether), your culture exists, it grows and it continues to evolve with the passage of time. It is the result of action and reaction. It is the lingering effect of every human interaction.

Change transformation is a complex undertaking. Sadly, many well-intended efforts to affect cultural change fail to meet the desired expectations. This happens, in part, because culture is addressed in silos, independent from strategy and capability. Maintaining cultural coherence across a company's portfolio must be an essential factor when determining a corporate strategy. No culture, however strong, can overcome poor choices when it comes to corporate strategy. No culture, however strong, can overcome ill-equipped capabilities. Strategy, capability and culture are the key trinity, three unique strands of the rope that must be woven together to effectively result in a successful change transformation. When effectively woven together, that proverbial rope is very difficult to break.

Performance more often comes down to a cultural challenge, rather than a technical one.

CULTURE IS KING

There are seven reasons that culture is sovereign over both strategy and capability:

1. **Loyalty.** People are loyal to culture, not to strategy or capability. You must be loyal to your employees (through a reliable and healthy corporate culture) to earn loyalty from your people, but this is a truth that many businesses don't embrace. Your workforce (team members) must know you consider them your greatest resource — that you never forget that, without them, value-add for customers and partners does not take place. Strategy, important as well, is a road map to get where you want to go. You must believe a loyal, committed team will take you there.

2. **Resiliency.** Culture provides resilience in tough times. Hard times, which we all know we cycle through sooner or later, may require a strategy adjustment. A committed, loyal team will insure the flexibility you need to navigate the "rocky shores."

3. **Efficiency.** Culture is more efficient than strategy and creates a competitive differentiation while providing a level of risk prevention that cannot be obtained with strategy. Loyal team members that have ownership in the culture are motivated to drive success into the business. They will constantly look for improvements to minimize cost and support efforts to design, launch and optimize technology. Further, they will embrace conceptually the need to possess a "competitive edge" to grow the business and opportunities for themselves and other team members.

4. **Complexity and strength.** When strategy and culture collide, culture will win. Our experience tells us that culture miscues are more damaging than strategic ones. If you believe that strategy is a plan, then you can appreciate that a plan can be adjusted, modified or changed as quickly as resources can be brought online to facilitate the "redirection." Culture is much more complex and takes time — requiring repeated reinforcement of values and creation of experiences to reinforce behaviors that provide results. By its very nature, culture building and sustainment must be more intentional.

5. **Uniqueness.** Strategies can be copied, but no one can copy your culture. Organizational culture is as unique as DNA. Although values and subsequent experiences may be somewhat standard, the actual profile of each organization's culture becomes unique based on the subtle differences of location, local demographics (including work ethic and traditions), work environment, characteristics of organizational leaders and customized tools to fit all the variables resident in different locations. It is my experience that the most effective way to build your organizational culture is to "cherry pick" best practices from successful suppliers, customers and any other business willing to share, and then customize those practices to fit your unique situation, considering all the variables mentioned above.

6. **Influence.** Culture provides greater discipline than disciplinary action does. Disciplinary action is an indicator of failure; needing it means you didn't select the right person, you didn't effectively train the right requirements, or you didn't provide effective tools and processes. A strong culture polices itself through ownership and commitment, a product of loyalty discussed in #1.

7. **Financial results.** Culture will have a significant impact on your future bottom line. This goes hand in hand with #3. When your team members take ownership for the success of the business, it will reflect proportionally in the bottom line. Culture is key to driving profitable growth.

Culture is the only sustainable competitive advantage that is completely within the control of its leader.

Chapter 4
RELATIONSHIP BETWEEN CULTURE AND VALUES

There are three elements to establishing a successful and sustainable continuous improvement program: *united values, aligned culture, and defined tools and competencies.* The previous chapter explored the importance of culture; now let's discuss its practical application.

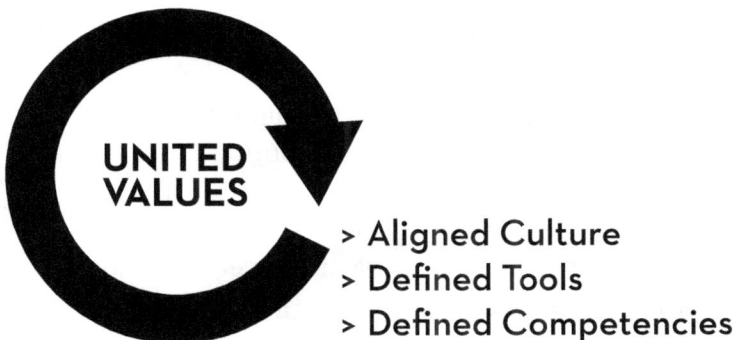

UNITED VALUES

> Aligned Culture
> Defined Tools
> Defined Competencies

Here is the simplest definition of organizational culture that I've applied in my own continuous improvement programs:

Culture is the environment shaped by the values that drive your decisions.

Don't overcomplicate the words; do understand the relationship. Your values drive your culture. Culture must never drive your values. Values become slave to the culture when they are undefined or unknown. In the absence of clear communication and indicated direction, negativity fills a vacuum. It is your job to align and clearly communicate whatever it is you are leading to your core values; everything else follows what is valued by the leader. If you are feeling the weight of this statement, good ... Welcome to leadership.

At my core, I am impatient, busy and direct. The older I get, the more impatient I grow with seemingly simple things that have been over-complicated by our modern day, efficient society. Does having a list of 60 or more passwords in your electronic wallet make you want to vomit? Mix in, to no fault of their own, a generation of employees who highly value their personal time and can summon an Uber driver in any state but may or may not have ever learned how to change their own car tire. That statement is not intended to offend, but to highlight the fact that speed-of-light technology advancements are influencing all generations and testing our core values as leaders and mentors. Boys and girls, life is hard, and generation and experience gaps are bigger than ever for manufacturing and service industries. All this sociological change, or rather opportunity, is at your front door, selling you Girl Scout cookies in a much smaller box.

The need to keep important things simple has never been more directly proportional to your success. If you can't explain your values, ideas and strategies at an eighth-grade level, you haven't invested enough time understanding the subject you are trying to communicate. Let's be honest — once the professor begins pontificating or the theologian starts quoting Greek or Latin on a Sunday morning, most of the guys I hang out with begin to study the back of their eyelids. People avoid complexity at all costs, so it's your job as a leader to keep things simple.

> The need to keep important things simple has never
> been more directly proportional to your success. If you
> can't explain your values, ideas and strategies at an
> eighth-grade level, you haven't invested enough time
> understanding the subject you are trying to communicate.

As I've said before, it's important to cherry-pick sources of material on this subject and apply them. The application will create personal retention; putting what is learned into practice becomes a habit. If you read a bunch of words and stories, it is all just entertainment, unless you can take away a tool and make it your own. (Be sure to check out all the Lean Tools offered in SECTION II of this book. There's much you can use, starting today on your lunch break.)

We have all heard leaders and seminars employ the KISS Method (Keep It Simple Stupid). Well, let's assume most people hired are not stupid, but I like the acronym, so I'll put a new spin on the phrase, *Keep It Simple, SMART!* The point is to keep things SIMPLE and that is a SMART management decision. Throughout my career, my colleagues and I have used the KISS acronym a lot. Keep things simple.

OPERATING FROM THE SAME PLAYBOOK

If you want everyone to get on the same page, begin by giving everyone the same book. As you consider your selection of Lean Manufacturing tools, don't get caught in the trap of implementing Japanese vocabulary, unless your employees speak Japanese. Keep the metrics and Key Production Indicator (KPI) formulas straightforward and simple. Tracking data on paper is not a sin of waste if the information is authentic and drives critical decisions. If you can automate data collection without drowning your organization in expensive man and machine computer systems, do so. Begin big, drill down; manual data collection must be visible, easy and looked at daily.

When the lead dog visits the fields of production, it should not be to simply sniff around and take a bio break, it should be to authentically gemba (go see and listen) to the people who add value to the organization. When this happens, it flips a switch on employee engagement. Data collected on a dirty, greasy fingerprinted form is of much greater value than a perfectly clean and mind-blowingly complex Excel OEE formulation that none of your employees can understand. It has been my experience that blended data points are confusing, often condescendingly academic, and expensive to maintain and not worth the paper they are printed on. If the guy and gal adding value to your production line don't see and understand the way their success is being measured, it is too complex. Keep things simple; keep things real ... *keep things real simple.*

If culture is an expression of the values used to make decisions, here is an example of why organizational values are the foundation of your company. A value, by simple definition, should be something of importance, worth, standards of behavior, and a reflection of what is important in life. I often ground my thinking in the simple truth: Organizations do not construct values, people do.

UNDERSTANDING THE DIFFERENCE BETWEEN CULTURE AND VALUES

Let me take you into two time-honored and traditionally established cultures — a bar on a Saturday night, and a place of worship on a Sunday morning.

We'll use these two settings to explore value and culture. As humans, we naturally confuse these important but elusive terms — value and culture. They are words rarely used in general business settings, until the HR department is needed, or someone hires a consultant. Most people have never seriously considered their own personal values and cultural inclinations. Only by looking in the rearview mirror across a lifetime of sorely won wisdom has it become easier for me to identify an organization whose leadership has not done the necessary work of understanding its core values. Equally, I find they have neglected the important work of honestly identifying the gap between established value and culture as it is actually lived out.

So let's go to the bar. *Keep in mind, it is at this sticky board room table that many critical business deals are made.* Relive a discussion you'd have at a bar with a colleague after work. I'm intentionally picking a bar setting to stress the importance of knowing your personal values and not confusing them with a fixed culture. In a bar setting, you might share some jokes, some colorful stories, engage in heated discussions about sports or politics, and wax philosophic about your personal aspirations, dreams and failures. Because a bar is relatively well-defined social setting, the bar culture can be immediately comfortable for some and uncomfortable for others. There is no clearly defined set of values within that culturally established environment. (There are values, but they are set by the owner trying to sell more food and drink at higher margins.) There is a clearly implied culture ... relax ... escape ... vent ... find pleasure. From a values viewpoint, the bar culture is neither good nor bad, it just is ... until its expression infringes on a personal or legal boundary.

By contrast, consider Sunday morning in a place of worship. Like the bar, a church environment is a well-defined social setting. The church can be immediately comfortable for some and uncomfortable for others. Let's imagine you are in Sunday school, at home around the dinner table, or engaged in a private more personal sharing with a close friend at a coffee shop. It could be a serious discussion, concerning society, your community, your health, even your personal convictions or aspirations.

What's the difference between the two discussions — the one at the bar and the one at church or the coffee shop? The cultural traditions (expressed as feelings) are associated with the setting, not our values.

We get into trouble ... in life, in relationships and, most significantly, in our organizations when hardcoded cultural traditions and cultural habits override or conflict with our values.

In a bar environment, you value camaraderie, relaxation and humor. At church, you value the sharing of personal human experience. The reason these two environments feel vastly different (and, in my opinion, shouldn't) is because deep down inside our hearts, where the real work of clearly defining what has worth, that work has not been done. Because many of us are not living out of our core value proposition, we may find ourselves behaving one way in a bar on Saturday night and another on Sunday morning in church.

Merriam-Webster calls this "hypocrisy" ... *Behavior that contradicts what one claims to believe or feel.*

Here is my point: A mature leader (or organization) must identify its bedrock core values. How you express them within different settings may be amplified or muted. What is valued remains and undergirds all significant actions and behaviors. Different social settings will have different traditions, but a person or culture with a branded value is liberated to operate within a wider range of cultural traditions. In other words, strong values create a fence of protection, protecting what is valued and keeping out what is not valued. Clearly defining these boundaries is an important issue: it is critical to the health of an organization, creating consistency and mapping behavioral terrain.

Strong values create a fence of protection, protecting what is valued and keeping out what is not valued.

MENTAL NOTE

If you do important things today, the urgent things of tomorrow never seem to arrive. If you don't know what is important, invest more time into understanding the root cause of the urgent, and you will soon discover what is important. Metaphorically, important things — like teenagers without enough positive distractions — become urgent things.

Have no doubt ... Your workplace will have pre-existing values. They may be silent, but they are there, nonetheless. The culture you feel is their offspring. This is especially challenging if you are a new leader in an existing workplace. You must first understand the current state of the culture, drill down into the values that are sustaining that culture and identify the leading positions that are keeping it in place. Developing future state value is pretty straightforward; killing the old is your challenge. Values are the root of culture and culture is the beginning of an effective continuous improvement program. Your core values are what drive what you do when nobody is looking. When you are working alone in your garage, do you behave the same as you would if the garage were full of friends or family? If you have team members working on an off shift, will they make the same decisions if management were present? The key to consistent behavior is value-driven behavior. I have found, and I believe you will find, defining and embracing values is the foundation for creating culture and effective continuous improvement.

If you can get people to adopt what the values are at work, and why you do things a certain way, you can get people to speak the same language about their work. If people come together, sharing a common understanding, intellectual talent can be leveraged. The same way we have fond recollections from social settings and touching memories from talking about our faith, we can make magic happen in the office. It's as simple as giving people a common understanding and common goals.

And before we get touchy-feely, let's remember that this is nothing more than making improvements. You are improving work in every possible sense. You're bringing your A-game, you're thinking big about what you're doing and you're giving people a chance to invest in their workplace. You're talking to people and engaging their minds. Your bottom line is bound to improve.

You might wonder how I got to be so certain about this.

I'm lucky because, even though I didn't realize the importance of values and culture until later in the game, it worked out anyway. In short, it's because I was creating a culture and didn't even know it until my organization reached a plateau in its progress. When we plateaued, and I then tried to figure out why we weren't improving any further, I discovered the concept of culture and its relationship to Continuous Improvement.

A great resource my colleagues and I found on this subject is the book *Change the Culture, Change the Game* by Roger Connors and Tom Smith. If you are serious about building an effective continuous improvement program, get a copy and read it. I've mentioned that I've read a lot of stuff on my culture journey; this is a book you should read cover-to-cover, and carefully. Don't skim it.

Had I understood the importance of organizational culture and how to influence it when I started our continuous improvement program, I'd have accelerated our success by several years. It would have made it easier for me to determine when we'd hit plateaus and then step the game up. Something to remember is that your continuous improvement success or organizational stability comes in plateaus and you have to recognize them so you know when to challenge the organization or step back and reinforce core values. The more finely you tune your ear to the cultural voice of your organization, the faster you self-correct, and the shorter your plateaus in growth will be.

> **Something to remember is that your continuous improvement success or organizational stability comes in plateaus and you have to recognize them so you know when to challenge the organization or step back and reinforce core values.**

The cultural anthropology of your organization reflects the norms and foundational values promoted by those holding power or responsibility. The members of any social group should be able to describe the norms, traditions, behaviors and results of their culture group. They may, however, be unable to define the unseen values that fostered a specific culture. This is an important part of the maturation of your team — them coming to understand the connection between the cause of value and effect of culture.

Chapter 5
THREE STAGES OF CULTURE

Early on, I envisioned that one of the objectives of our Continuous Improvement program was to build personal accountability. Once I became aware of the three stages of culture, which I'll outline in this chapter, it became possible to measure how far the program had come. Accountability will be discussed in full later, but let it be stated here that "accountability" will be manifested in how enthusiastic and self-directing your team members become. If they can assign responsibility and take action on their own, your CI program is doing well.

As I mentioned before, you will likely experience plateaus, "stair steps" if you will, in the course of your continuous improvement program. I will offer specific suggestions for how to improve your own company's Continuous Improvement culture later. For now, embrace the concept that, if you understand the stages of culture, you can monitor your progress and know when it's time to implement the next steps, which will continually improve your Continuous Improvement culture.

As I began to discover and define the concept of culture, I learned from some experts in the safety industry that there are three stages of culture:

Stage One: The team member says, "The Company is responsible for me."

Stage Two: The team member says, "I am responsible for myself."

Stage Three: The team member says, "I am responsible for my fellow team member."

Reaching Stage Three will represent the ultimate maturation of your organization. This should be one of the top objectives of your own CI program.

If you look at Chapter 7: Give Culture a Name!, you'll see a reference to "The Oz Principle." This concept is a theme that can be used to eliminate "victimization" (the blame game) and elevate team problem solving to focus on identifying, owning, developing solutions and executing. Stage Two of culture is apparent when your team members take ownership for their actions. Once your teams willingly work together to solve issues that impede the team's ability to maximize their contribution to gain sharing, you know you have achieved the second the stage of culture.

The third stage of culture is, although the ultimate goal, rarely achieved by most teams. An organization at this stage has adopted the idea of continuous improvement and applied the concept to daily operations. There is a strong emphasis on communications, training, management style, and improving efficiency and effectiveness. Everyone in the organization can contribute. Team members understand the impact of behavioral issues on CI. The level of awareness of behavioral and attitudinal issues is high, and measures are being taken to improve behavior. Progress is made one step at a time and never stops. The organization asks how it might help others.

For an organization that develops the third stage of culture continuously, the following characteristics may be observed:

- CI and production efforts are equally valued.
- CI organizations focus on the longer term as well as the present.
- Problems and root causes are addressed before becoming systemic.
- Short-term performance is measured and stabilized early on, ensuring long-term success.
- Metrics (KPIs) are simple and trusted.
- Collaboration in both word and deed at all levels.
- Culture must have a name or a readily identified brand.
- CI is never sacrificed in pursuit of production targets.
- People individually are respected and valued for their contributions.
- Errors are viewed as opportunities to reduce process variability – not head count.
- Conflict is recognized as passion and dealt with by encouraging mutual solutions.
- Managers live CI by being listeners, coaches, trainers and process improvers.
- Continuous Learning is synonymous with Continuous Improvement.
- Time is motion, and motion is laden with waste, eliminating waste is highly valued.
- Relationships are paramount; there is no distinction between the internal and external customer(s).
- Leaders and workers at all levels are aware of the impact of cultural values, and these are key decision drivers.
- The organization rewards producers and supporters of producers.

The three stages of evolution of culture ("The company is responsible for me," "I am responsible for myself," and "I am responsible for my fellow team member") are clearly relevant to any team-based, value-added operation. Large-scale organizations present challenges on ensuring that there are good communications and cooperation between the various functions within the organization. Communications tend to be more direct in smaller groups. The response to pressure from peers is likely to be quicker in small groups, but partially countering this is the potential influence that the culture of a professional institution can have on individuals within these groups.

The process for the development of CI culture can be assisted by the use of a training process within an organization. A person or organization learns by reflecting on what they have experienced, formulating concepts and ideas for change while continuing existing best practices.

The timeline required to progress through the various stages of development in any organization or industry cannot be predicted. Much will depend upon the circumstance of an individual organization and the commitment and effort that it devotes to effect change. Historical experience to date indicates that the timeframe for change can be long, but it should be recognized that many of the organizational concepts that have provided a new perspective on the influence of culture on CI have only been conceived in recent years. Now that these concepts and supporting principles are acknowledged internationally, and practical experience is being shared, it may well be possible to progress through the stages more rapidly. However, sufficient time must be taken in each stage to allow the benefits from changed practices to be realized and to mature. Team members and management must be prepared for such change.

PERSONAL ACCOUNTABILITY

Management consultant Todd Herman defined personal account-ability as "being willing to answer — to be accountable — for the outcomes resulting from your choices, behaviors and actions." When you're personally accountable, you take ownership of situations that you're involved in.

When I was 26 years young, I was stationed outside of Frankfurt, Germany in a remote munitions-storage facility storing tactical warheads. I was standing on the end of the earth on Christmas Eve. I missed America, my family and all things kind. Green is a mild way to describe what I was, a first lieutenant in the U.S. Army, stationed far from everything familiar. As part of a military management team, we were responsible for the maintenance and security of weapons systems that would be used as our first line of defense. Due to the characteristics of the highly destructive materials for which we were responsible, we were positioned in a remote lonely location. This added to the angst of feeling like we were no longer in Kansas. As you can imagine, being in the post-Vietnam military culture, home-sickness and low morale was our daily bread. In this environment, personal accountability was imperative.

This environment drives and exhausts you into the deepest reserves of personal accountability. You want to be angry, commanding, but understanding what the human spirit really needs is empathy and concern. Pain will bring people to action, but only for a season; empathic leadership will make people go through a wall for you. This emotional intelligence cannot be fabricated; it is organic. You basically must feel pain before other people do. This makes for great personal accountability.

> Pain will bring people to action, but only
> for a season; empathic leadership will make
> people go through a wall for you.

On Christmas Eve, I knew my young troops were thinking about home because I was too. Fifteen of my young men, most of them just 18 years old, were alone and rotating in one-man guard posts. The air was bitter cold, frozen and depressing. I was consumed by empathy, I felt compelled to provide comfort to relieve some of the homesickness, in them and me. So I packed up homemade cookies, baked by my bride and walked to each post, I quickly gave a wrapped can of cookies to each soldier. Most importantly, I looked in their eyes and thanked them for giving part of their life energy to serve a post that most Americans did not know existed. I pumped their hands in mine and told each man this simple truth: they were a man, they were American and they were appreciated. I thanked them and gave them a vision of what they meant to those at home, whose freedom they were guarding. This is personal accountability. They taught me more that night about values and dedication than I can share in this space.

In the manufacturing culture in which I worked and led, we continuously talked about the need for and importance of personal accountability. In his article "Personal Accountability and the Pursuit of Workplace Happiness," Cy Wakeman, suggests that you work to bulletproof your people instead of attempting to make their world a cozier place. Once they stop focusing on what's happening "to" them and focus on what they can do within their current circumstances to succeed, they will get the results they are looking for. These results will lead to a happier, more engaged attitude — particularly at work — as it will reaffirm that they are the architects of their own lives and can handle whatever comes their way. Once they realize how competent they are, a greater confidence in their abilities will follow.

The article points to four factors that contribute directly to personal accountability: commitment, resilience, ownership and continuous learning.

The concept of personal accountability is central to the creation of a continuous improvement culture. It should be considered as one of the key values embraced to build the helix of culture.

THE DECEPTION OF LEAPS AND BOUNDS

My co-author, Susan, and her family have gone on several annual pilgrimages to an indoor swimming park outside of Cincinnati, Ohio. If you have ever visited an indoor water park in the dead of winter, you remember it. If you've never had the pleasure, just picture a tropical indoor amusement park powered by rushing water. These parks are filled with blurry-eyed parents and hyped-up kids skidding across wet pavement, boats whooshing down waterfalls, costumed characters pushing everything from pelleted ice cream to Bud Lite. This chlorine-scented, pizza-sauced vacation is Heaven-on-Earth for any red-blooded 8-year-old.

Susan's family was particularly excited about challenging one another in the Lily Pad Pond (though I'm sure the kids were more excited than the adults!). The annual Olympic-worthy event required each contender to cross the pool, by way of lily pad, not water. Over the years, Susan had seen many unique strategies employed to traverse the pond of death. The best natural crosser she ever witnessed was a fearless 60-pound kid, running the gauntlet by stepping on the center of the lily pads. Most adults believe they, too, can channel their inner flying squirrel technique, but gravity always wins. Susan's own flying squirrels were determined to teach the entire family how to successfully cross the lily pond, and they would not stop until *all* of them had crossed the pond without falling into the water.

After many failed attempts, Susan learned that leaps and bounds did not bring progress. Only by working together, floating the pads closer to one another and helping each other crawl across the pads, could they claim Team Gold!

Just like crossing the lily pad pond, in business, there is a flawed notion that great progress happens in leaps and bounds. This is an organizational deception that we all must overcome. Real progress starts and ends with teams committing to taking one step at a time, *together.* It feels counter intuitive, even painful, to intentionally slow our own progress to help another catch up. After all, the goal is to speed up, right? *Wrong!* The ultimate goal is team progress ... *sustained team progress.* This requires a greater vision and organizational discipline. It is not our nature to help another's success, but sustainable progress demands we do exactly that — help one another for the greater win of advancing together. Leave no team member behind.

Earlier in this chapter, I introduced the three stages of culture, and you'll remember that stage 3 inspires employees to operate with the attitude "I am responsible for my fellow team member's success." Those who adopt that team-based attitude and then understand the deception of "leaps and bounds" are those who are poised for true, sustainable success. Knowing this, we relaunched at RFC what we called STEPS Team Structures. Some of the teams were larger and met as smaller subgroups during their individual shifts. What was unique about the way we managed the teams was that all square footage in all locations was divided into numbered "zones." Every Zone had a named Champion and/or a Team Coordinator, and was visited quarterly to ensure the Zone was progressing in what we called 6S stability (a lean tool described in detail in Section II of this book).

When we introduced these changes at RFC, we did so intentionally. Traditional audits were suddenly called "reports," and staff members started focusing on listening and connecting to resource needs, rather than grading teams. What had been called CI Teams became "STEPS Teams," and we returned to our roots by linking what we called our STEPS Bonus and STEPS Training programs to our team names. (At the company, STEPS was an acronym that stood for "Successful Team Effort Provides Satisfied Customers.") As the STEPS Teams culture rolled out, we added a monthly Safety Observation and quarterly self-conducted 6S Report Card activity to continually protect our most valued resource: our team members. Providing for and protecting our most valued resource meant that we would be visibly organized and intentionally observant of our working environment. We were building a culture in which we succeeded together. Looking back on this transition, I am so proud of my colleagues. I knew, at the time, that it was within the essence and culture of the RFC employee to jump into the deep end and help others cross to success, and that is what made our proverbial pond a remarkable workplace filled with extraordinary people.

Chapter 6
Cultural DNA

Organizational culture is the product of the values used to make decisions. Therefore, if you want to change or create a new result, you must first change or create new organizational values. Once values are "clearly mapped" by organizational leaders, the formula for changing culture becomes simple. Leaders create experiences that reinforce beliefs that drive actions, which yield improved results and future performance.

> **Leaders create experiences that reinforce beliefs that drive actions, which yield improved results and FUTURE PERFORMANCE.**

So many of us know the Results Pyramid model introduced by Roger Connors and Tom Smith in their cornerstone book, *Change the Culture, Change the Game.* Over time, my team and I built upon those concepts and developed our own model, which we call cultural DNA or the CI Helix.

Picture this dynamic as a DNA helix chain; I call it the Continuous Improvement Helix (CI Helix). If you want to move your organization from its current performance to a new improved performance, you must first take a hard look at your total organizational DNA,

FUTURE PERFORMANCE

VALUES

- Results
- Actions
- Beliefs
- Experiences

VALUES

- Results
- Actions
- Beliefs
- Experiences

VALUES

- Results
- Actions
- Beliefs
- Experiences

VALUES

CURRENT PERFORMANCE

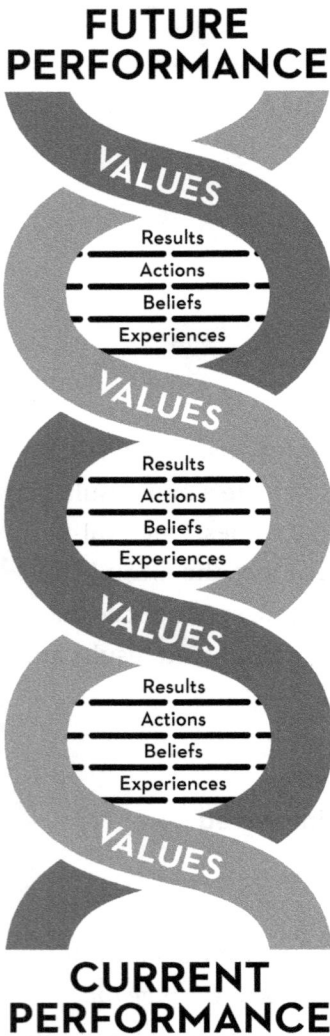

The CI Helix, ©2019, Ray Leathers

which includes values, experiences, beliefs, actions and results (visible characteristics).

DNA (deoxyribonucleic acid) is a two-chain molecule that possesses the mysteriously distinctive and unchanging characteristics that define humans and most other organisms. And DNA is the perfect metaphor for organizations too, as the genetic blueprint, so to speak, of any given company is unique, pervasive and predicts how the organization will function. As such, it should be what I call a "top button issue" for leaders to recognize their own organizational DNA output at all levels of the organization.

Here is where the hard work comes in … really knowing, *seeing* your organizational DNA outside of your own paradigm or biased filters. This is much more than writing down a list of lofty values in a staff meeting and establishing KPIs. Truly knowing your organizational DNA requires that you invest and examine the resulting characteristics of your values at all levels, and that you relentlessly demand the good folks chained to you to do the same. When cultural values are obvious and unchanging, your DNA will affect people's experiences. These consistent experiential inputs (people are always looking for input) will drive repeated or predictable beliefs.

These beliefs will result in the actions (decisions) that yield desired performance and results.

> Truly knowing your organizational DNA requires that you invest and examine the resulting characteristics of your values at all levels, and that you relentlessly demand the good folks chained to you to do the same.

You will never know if your cultural DNA is being proliferated from generation to generation unless you honestly (sometimes painfully) observe and measure the yield from your newest, youngest or most vulnerable additions to your organization. As such, your new hires are a great place to begin observations. Organizational self-awareness is critical to your success and or failure. The course of every employee behavior will line up behind the intentional or unintentional experiences your values drive.

AN IDENTITY BUILT UPON VALUES

The CI Helix is the culture of continuous improvement, designed to carry you from current to future performance. In this model, the vertical strands that connect the rungs or steps of the helix structure are your organizational values. To climb the helix ladder (i.e., to change the culture), you must create experiences that reinforce beliefs, which drive actions that improve results. Put another way, your employees need to (a) feel something that (b) affects what they do (c) in a way that makes them think and adjust, and (d) ultimately impacts the bottom line.

> Your employees need to feel something that affects what they do in a way that makes them think and adjust, and ultimately impacts the bottom line.

Here's a concrete example. I come from the metal-working industry. Metal is a valuable resource. Therefore, scrap — or leftover, useless metal — is a problem. It's waste. The more scrap we have, the less profit we have.

> **"Stop swatting flies and go after the manure pile."**
>
> — *General Curtis LeMay*

Knowing this, we designed a system to track scrap. It could be tracked by our operators and would be reported on a monthly basis. We told them that we wanted to be more efficient, that we wanted to reduce scrap and that we'd be monitoring the numbers on a month-to-month basis. Any time we did not see an improvement from one month to the next, we required a "root cause/corrective action analysis" by the production team (a fancy way of saying "Why is there more scrap, and how, exactly, are you going to reduce it?"). Management would help them correct the problem by giving direction and offering any resources they needed to cut down on waste.

Once our operators understood that management would help them, and that their compensation would go up when scrap went down, they became more deliberate. They self-reinforced certain behaviors. During a three-year period, our scrap went down by 50 percent. That's huge!

You might say that this is squeezing results out of your employees, or paying them off to do better work. I say, *nay*. It is neither of those things. Although we might be looking at day-to-day numbers in concrete ways, this practice ultimately has everything to do with values and culture. Why do I say so?

Number one: It was not purely a matter of incentives. It was not simply a choice between "lose your job by doing poorly" or "make more money by doing better." We weren't threatening them, and we weren't bribing them. We were telling them what we wanted. We were saying what the values were. And in this case, we highly valued efficiency and our shared job security.

Number two: We were helping them buy into the values. We were asking them: "What do you need? What questions do you have? How can we help?" They're the operators, so they know quite a bit, including the parts of their process that need more attention. By being team players for them, they could become team players for us, at which point it was only fair that they should share in the wealth. A rising tide lifts all boats. If everyone is efficient, everyone wins. And please tell me what's better than a company in which everyone has an equal interest in doing better?

> "Educating the mind without educating the heart is no education at all."
>
> — *Aristotle*

To return to the CI Helix ladder, remember that the operators (a) felt a need to be efficient, which (b) made them be more careful, which meant that (c) they were thinking in terms of scrap/waste, which (d) improved our bottom line.

Notice that values come at the beginning of that process. In this case, "efficiency" is the value. It's the first thought we wanted the operators to have, at the beginning of everything they do in their daily work. Once we *told them* that efficiency was the value, they folded it into their experience. They were thinking in terms of efficiency. "How can this be quicker? How can I generate less scrap?"

Sometimes, all you must do is ask. "Hey, we're trying to make things more efficient, and that means cutting down on scrap. Could you take a stab at it?"

For now, it's that simple.

CHANGE THE CULTURE, CHANGE THE RESULTS

To change (or create) your culture, you have to start by identifying things that need to change. Only then can you say what results you want to improve — and following that, what people will have to do to bring about those better results.

> To change (or create) your culture, you have to start by identifying things that need to change.

The changes will probably be small. Let me repeat that: *The changes will probably be small.* Business will continue as usual; whatever your people do, they will continue to do it. Think of your people as football players, and remember that you're not trying to convert kickers into linemen; you're just trying to make better kickers. Still, as any football kicker with good coaching will tell you, small changes make a huge difference. They make a difference in yards. If you challenge people and give them a metric by which to measure progress — the way that you could give a kicker yards to measure their own progress — you could see tremendous improvement.

I suspect you can probably see what role the right Lean tools will play later: in short, they'll give people something to work with toward the goal. But it starts with culture. Make your people believe. Or better yet, give them something to believe in.

> **Make your people believe. Or better yet, give them something to believe in.**

In Chapter 4, we talked about the cultural concepts of a bar on a Saturday night and a church on Sunday morning. In the end, however, you don't have to be their bar buddy or their minister. You just have to play your part at work. Set the values accordingly. Give them something to believe in, some standard to strive for. If it's your value as a manager, it can be theirs as an employee. And none of this has to be touchy-feely. If you tell them that you want to sell more, or market more, or be more efficient, they will believe it and work with you — if you tell them, and if you tell them why.

I should mention that you don't necessarily need to roll out only one initiative at a time. You can be working on several different things, so long as all of them get attention. We implemented our scrap reduction initiative while we undertook our quality improvement, time-delivery and time-efficiency initiatives. And they all worked!

Change the culture, change the results. This is how you start building your own culture, SO SHUT UP AND GET LEAN!

Chapter 7
GIVE CULTURE A NAME!

When I realized I needed to launch some sort of effort to "turn around" our company, I still hadn't realized a few things that now seem obvious. In the first place, I didn't realize right away that it was going to be a journey of continuous improvement (CI). But I also didn't know that I was asking myself to change a company's culture and, worse, I honestly wasn't thinking of company culture much at all.

But I started down this path anyway, looking for the right footholds, and the first place I stopped was at values. I stopped there because I'd been wondering about something: What is it like when there aren't supervisors watching? What drives behavior when employees don't feel like they have to "act the part" for someone watching?

> What is it like when there aren't supervisors watching? What drives behavior when employees don't feel like they have to "act the part" for someone watching?

As I've said, it's really a question of values. I knew that employees could do their jobs for a dozen reasons, and I knew that, as a leader, I could elevate their thinking about work. Conveniently, value talk is easy if you're being straight with people. There's no need to reinvent the wheel — people will already know what you're talking about. To start, all you have to do is *identify* your company's values and give some context.

If you're in a position of responsibility, I'd guess you spend a good deal of time at work reading and analyzing and thinking about high-level stuff. Have you turned it inward and thought about *why* you do what you do at work? Have you put names to those values? And if they're working well for you, how do you pass them on? (If you don't feel like it's working, you're not alone. Keep reading.)

Identifying values is a foundational experience. It's very simple, but very important. Equally important is giving your cultural makeover a name. After all, if this is the language you want people to be speaking, it needs to be easy to speak.

At RFC, our continuous improvement culture was called STEPS ("Successful Team Effort Provides Satisfied Customers"). We implemented a "STEPS Bonus" gain-sharing program that paid out a bonus to every employee in the company on a quarterly basis. For us, it was an all-encompassing machine with a name — and a direct link in employees' minds between our company values, their work and their income. One reason that's useful is that, with people making those mental connections, they're much more likely to see the point of communications, training, metrics and new tools, and they're much quicker to embrace them.

Your CI program, and the culture that results, may not have gain-sharing as an option. However, you can still connect company values to some direct benefit to the team — the company's survival and the individual's job security, keeping key customers, opportunities for growth, and so forth. Again, having a name makes it easier for the idea to stick, and a name will therefore also make it easier to leverage this for everyone's benefit.

PROBLEM-SOLVING AND CONFLICT

Aside from your continuous improvement program as a whole, you may find occasion to give values — or the way they manifest at your company — names and themes of their own. As another example, one of our first struggles in the implementation of a CI program was problem-solving and conflict. There had been a good deal of finger-pointing, blame and the all-too-common "that's not my job" talk. Luckily, I was introduced to *The Oz Principle*, a book by Roger Connors, which I now highly recommend to you.

The Oz Principle first points out what is "below the line," namely those same problems typical among untrained and undisciplined workers (finger-pointing and so forth). Connors then teaches readers how to take a situation "above the line" by using the virtues of the four characters from the film *The Wizard of Oz*.

You must:

1. Have the Lion's Courage to see the problem.
2. Have the Tin Man's Heart to take ownership of the problem.
3. Have the Scarecrow's Brain to solve the problem.
4. Have Dorothy's conviction to execute and follow through.

We decided to train our CI teams on this principle for problem-solving purposes. And with that decision, "let's take it above the line" became a common phrase in meetings, and conflict resolution was suddenly much less of a headache!

In any case, whatever your company's needs, whatever program you design and whatever values you adhere to, call them what they are — and give your efforts a new name so it can truly come alive.

Chapter 8
THE HAWTHORNE EFFECT

We'll spend a great deal of time talking about specific tools later on, but while we're knee-deep in a discussion of company culture and values, there's one indispensable tool to introduce, and that tool (or principle) is called the Hawthorne effect.

Put simply, the Hawthorne effect is this: The employees watch what the boss watches.

The term "the Hawthorne effect" was coined in 1950 by a researcher named Henry Landsberger while he was studying experiments conducted earlier at the Hawthorne Works, a Western Electric factory outside of Chicago. When they were conducted, the experiments aimed to find out whether factory workers performed better under different lighting conditions.

During the changes in lighting, worker performance went up across the board, but only for as long as the experiment was conducted; worker productivity dropped back off when the experiment was over. Landsberger concluded, from the available evidence, that the main factor causing an increase in performance was observation. Workers were aware that the bosses were watching, that the bosses were taking an interest in their performance and in their workspace, and they responded accordingly.

There is a behaviorist side to this, of course; everyone knows that there are sticks and carrots at work. But this isn't about surveillance *per se*; it really is about sharing your vision. I say so because, for workers to do particularly well at their jobs, they have to know what you're looking for!

The workers watch what the boss watches.

Watching waste? Tell your employees that you want to reduce waste overall, and you want to see their contribution to it drop. They'll know to be less wasteful.

Watching turnaround times? Tell your employees that you want to see the times tighten and you want them to be models for an efficient system. They'll know to be more efficient.

Watching customer satisfaction ratings? Tell your employees that you want to see the happiest customers that commerce can produce, starting today. Remind them how important that is for business and how important their job is in making customers happy. They'll think to be friendly, helpful and professional more than they've ever thought about it before.

You watch these things and *tell employees* what you're watching, and they will be better able to show you what you want to see. Who knows? You might even find some of your brightest stars and best innovators come out of obscurity once you issue such challenges.

But be aware — you *can* overdo it. You don't want to overwhelm them with a ton of new initiatives — it would only water down what you can expect from it. As our old rule goes, KISS — Keep It Simple, Smartie! The Hawthorne effect won't do anything if the people doing the work don't understand what you're looking for, or can't fully engage themselves with it.

Identify what's important, find a simple way to track it and then take some action to make changes. Share with everyone what you're watching and why. If you can then find a way to reward good performance — to give everyone a boost when they do a good job — you've got a winning formula. Because aside from having a booming, profitable business, you're also starting to build a culture of high-quality work that will sustain itself even when you're not observing the floor.

Chapter 9
Building Attitudes Is Building Culture

If I wanted to, I could make a perfectly healthy employee feel ill. It wouldn't require foul play of any kind. Want to know how I'd do it?

Picture this. I walk out of my office, through the honeycomb of desks right outside my door and, as I'm walking, I start to pass an employee ... we'll call him Dave. He says hi to me. As he does, I stop in my tracks and look at him just a little bit cock-eyed.

> **RAY:** "Hey, Dave. Say, are you feeling all right?"

> **DAVE:** "I think so. Why?"

> **RAY:** "You just ... you're paler than usual. You look like you could use a lozenge, or maybe some aspirin."

> **DAVE:** "I ... well, that's weird. I feel fine."

> **RAY (concerned):** "Well, for some reason, you don't *look* fine. You having any aches? A headache? A fever?"

> **DAVE:** "No. Well, not that I know of, anyway."

> **RAY:** "All right, if you say so. Keep an eye on it for me, will you? You know how things tend to go around."

> **DAVE (now nervous):** "O-okay, Ray."

Before bumping into me, Dave might have been in excellent spirits, but now he wonders if he could have caught something from his child, from his wife, or from a co-worker. He's running his tongue over the roof of his mouth and checking his forehead with the back of his hand. Ten bucks says that, if he happens to get a headache around dinnertime, he calls in sick the next day just to be sure. If he were particularly affected by my acting, it's legitimately possible that he would *become* sick though he wouldn't have otherwise.

My little stunt would work because of the power of suggestion, to which none of us are fully immune. But it wouldn't be a harmless prank, like pointing at the floor and telling someone they dropped their arm. Dave is now feeling unwell, and it's anyone's guess if he shows up to work tomorrow. That affects what we can do as a company. And Dave is one of many, many employees in an organization where the well-being of our people has huge implications for our success as a company.

I use this example to show how important — and immediate — the effects of attitude are. Never mind illness; what I did was an exercise in attitude choice. For one minute, I chose to be nervous, paranoid, prying; Dave merely picked up on it. Any of us would.

In the book *It's Your Ship*, Navy Captain D. Michael Abrashoff explained that, while living aboard a military vessel, he would be especially cranky the next day if he'd been deprived of sleep, which usually happened if he was called multiple times during the night. Eventually he learned that the crew would size up his mood and attitude at 6:00 a.m. reveille, and the word would quickly spread around the ship if he had a bad attitude. "The dark side is out," they'd murmur to one another. Because those midnight calls were necessary, and the tired crankiness was unavoidable, he learned to keep more to himself on such days, and the mood of the crew seemed consistently better after that.

Military officer or civilian leader, if you're the boss and you're in a bad mood, you can ruin *everyone's* day. No one is comfortable when the boss is in a bad mood. But it gets worse. The same way that I robbed my own company of productivity by suggesting to Dave he felt sick, I can rob my company just by being a sourpuss. If you think the boss doesn't care about you, is unpleasant to be around and is never pleased with anything you do, what reason do you have to try?

No one is comfortable when the boss is in a bad mood.

But what is wonderful about attitude — and human beings, really — is that we have the capacity to choose. Things do happen, and all of us wake up on the wrong side of the bed sometimes. But when I walk into the office, it isn't about me, or the fact that I might be in a bad mood. I'm the boss, I like what I do and I want everyone to have a good day of work. So, I'm going to act the part!

This takes practice. It's a daily exercise, and it starts with little things. Work on it a while, and then the true test will come. You'll encounter something that challenges your mood significantly — injury, illness, trouble at home, bad news at the office. You'll be overwhelmed, and one of your employees will ask, "Hey, how are you?"

The correct answer: You're doing all right, thanks! You're happy to see everyone. At a bare minimum, you're "fine" — but if that's the answer you choose, please try to sound like you mean it. People will see it, take note of it and they'll wonder how you do it. (You choose it.) As with anything else, they'll model a good example if given one.

Attitude has a huge impact on communication. And communication is an important subject to understand for CI undertakings of any size or flavor. Communication (with the right attitude) is one of the biggest parts of your job in a CI program, so get to a mirror and check yourself.

ATTITUDES ARE CONTAGIOUS ...
IS YOURS WORTH CATCHING?

> No one can sustainably follow a negative leader.

I have learned that one of the keys to culture is the bravado, cadence and attitude of a leader. I have found this is critical to your organizational success or failure. No one can sustainably follow a negative leader. It doesn't matter how you feel as the leader. Sorry to burst your bubble. It is your job to be the leader by doing the right things and by demonstrating the right attitudes — attitudes worth emulating. When you agreed to take compensation and title for a leader's level of risk and life energy, you relinquished your license to tantrum. You must die to the selfish and immature desire to express your own feelings if those feelings don't serve the company and its people. Your *mood* must become secondary to the importance of how your troops feel.

Fake it 'til you make it.

Bravado, cadence and attitude are contagious. Let me give you an example. On the way to work on a cold, windy, rainy, winter morning, you get a flat tire. You pull over on the interstate to change the tire (you don't have AAA or road service). As you get out, other cars and trucks are screaming by at 70 mph, blowing a wet combination of mist and road dirt all over you. You finally dig the spare tire out of the trunk and, after an inordinate amount of time, you locate the jack. It takes forever to get the hubcap off, and getting down on your knees (soaking your pants), you finally figure out how to place the jack under the car so it doesn't fall off after you remove the flat tire.

While loosening the lugs, the cheap multi-purpose wrench slips off the over-tightened nut, smashing your knuckle. Soaked, cold, wet and covered with road dirt, you manage with great difficulty to get the spare on; you put the wet, nasty flat tire and jack back in the trunk and make your way to work. Now you've got to figure out how and when to get the flat tire repaired and back on the car, you have a fully packed schedule, and your spouse needs the car to take the kids on a school field trip tomorrow.

You enter the door at the office, knuckle screaming, soaking wet and covered with road dirt. Just when you thought you had cleared the entry gauntlet without catching another stone, the quality control technician (who chides you daily about the importance of enthusiasm) shouts, "Good Morning! How are you on this beautiful day?"

What is your likely response? It would feel really good to just let that person standing before you, forcing your response, to get the full brunt of your highly flammable morning napalm.

Within that tiny space of stimulus and response lies a critically important decision that only you own. Do you give away your personal power or claim power over your behavior? It is within this space that either leaders or victims are revealed — the attitude we chose actualizes our ultimate reality. How we behave after receiving stimulus (positive or negative) is both habit forming and, most importantly, life defining. Our habitual responses to stimuli ultimately define us.

The good news is God gave you the ability to reason, the only living being in His Kingdom with this gift. You know attitude is contagious, you know your responsibility as a leader (at work and at home), so you park your car, you turn off the engine, you place your hands on the steering wheel, and you remind yourself of the potential impact of your attitude on others and on your own response patterns. You make the commitment to yourself that no one will be affected by the previous events of your day. You utilize your God-given ability to reason, adjust your attitude and empower your leader values.

Gut checking is the work of a lone-wolf leader, ensuring that you are not subconsciously playing the role of a victim is a private character victory over the response 'space' monster that invites you to throw adult temper tantrums.

When you walk through the door and choose humor, positive words, open body language, self-mastery, you inoculate your colleagues and family with those same attitudes. You are intentionally changing both their atmosphere and your own. That is real power! Way more powerful and enticing and attractive than force, might and misdirected frustration. Why poison the people that will make you successful at work, or the people you love at home with a negative, downtrodden attitude that makes life's paradigm chaotic and stressful?

Looking back over 40 years of experience, I have seen countless professional engineers, military leaders and executives give away their personal power by habitually expressing hopelessness, negativity and offering silence to their subordinates. *These emotional responses are the three dark riders of the leader's apocalypse.*

If you walk the fields of production, greeting your employees, sincerely asking them about their families, work, even financial challenges, you will see and feel the importance of your role as their leader. I am not coaching you to be false; I am coaching you to grow up and check your own mood at the door, so you can authentically encourage and prepare to give real hope to your employees. By sincerely listening and providing real encouragement, you will be personally strengthened. By giving your authentic attention to employees, you will receive sanction and respect from the 'boots on the ground.' That is an endorsement you cannot lead without. You will also hear things that your senior staff and lieutenants kindly protected your ears from hearing. Connecting to your employees is the most important thing you will do all day long. It is at this intersection that both leader and follower walk together.

As you will see elsewhere in this book, I have learned two golden rules about culture in my years of management: (1) it's all about the leader and (2) people watch what the bosses watch. This applies to Rule 1 — it's all about the leader. If you're going to be a leader, be a good one; your culture depends on it!

Chapter 10

Launching Your Continuous Improvement System

I've talked a great deal about the importance of culture in creating and sustaining an effective CI program. But now let's turn our attention to some of the tools and methodology that brought my organization to the peak of industry performance. Where before I've discussed culture, and how it works invisibly, I'll start taking more time to discuss the parts that work visibly as well — things like tools, keys, rules and the results one can expect.

I realized early in the planning process for our continuous improvement program that it would be challenging to design tools that help people do their jobs better in measurable ways. In particular, I had to design tools that would work to advance the value I'd decided was most important: accountability. And when I say I had to "design tools" for accountability, it ultimately means I had to create an experience that reinforced accountable behavior. Let's just say that there were a few "trials" before we managed to launch the following key items:

Manufacturing and Office Continuous Improvement (CI) Teams were designated in each dedicated value-stream, such as a production cell (e.g., assembly or machine operation department) or functional support team (e.g., sales, human resources or engineering). Teams were minimized to fewer than 10 team members. The teams were required to measure and track metrics that we know impact profitability; therefore, manufacturing teams would track data like scrap, rejects and efficiency while the office teams would have to identify (and then track) two other metrics that impact profits.

CI Boards were established in each team's area and were required to display (at a minimum) the standardized forms for tracking team metrics, the minutes of team meetings, any CI projects (resulting from any incidence of a "root cause/corrective action" [RC/CA] item), previous quarter report cards and CI savings created by certain projects. I did find it necessary to differentiate between CI and 5S/6S projects (see more on 6S in Section II of this book); this allows you to drive CI implementation through RC/CA with focus on 5S (note that 5S will lose priority over CI projects if not differentiated). Teams could decorate and display other forms, reports, pictures or other materials that supported team efforts, successes, morale or celebration. Although we did stick closely to our standardized program forms, we encouraged people to put unique touches in the spirit of playful competition.

Standardized Team Meetings were conducted twice per month. A standard meeting agenda form was provided to guide those team meetings (because, as you surely know, most people don't know how to conduct a good meeting). The first of those two monthly meetings is held so the team can review their metrics from the previous month and start the Root Cause/Corrective Action ball rolling as needed — and that's for any place where the team didn't see continuous improvement. As many RC/CA inquiries create projects, the second monthly team meeting is to follow up on RC/CA and any projects that have sprung from it. (The effectiveness of these meetings is one of the subjective factors audited as described below.)

Senior staff would audit every CI team every quarter. Two members of my senior staff would schedule these audits in advance. We developed a standardized audit form (a "report card") and used it to ensure comprehensive, even-handed audits were conducted (as even senior managers will sway widely when not given a standard to follow). At the end, the report card provided an objective score (which was based on the measurable data) and a subjective score (which was based on evidence of the team's commitment and effort). Every team was given a printed copy of their quarterly report card, and every team was required to display it on their team's CI board (also checked during the subsequent audit). These audits were then used to reward the best CI team in each plant and the office every quarter. Winning teams got to present their successes at quarterly rallies, they received a modest reward like a gift card or lunch, or perhaps some company outerwear.

What you notice is that the CI projects become the centerpiece of this program, and that's where real improvement happens in the company. That's where innovation is at its peak. That's where employees realize that they're actually important.

Visit www.CIhelix.com to download sample forms.

As I mentioned in Chapter 7, we developed a gain-sharing "bonus" through which all employees participated on an equal basis. The gain-sharing program was a simple method to provide all team members the capability to share in the success of the continuous improvements they implemented. One challenge in the implementation of change is the perceived or real benefit derived by the participants in the organization that must drive the change. I suggest that the speed and effectiveness of change will be in a direct ratio with the motivation of those implementing the change. Management has used infinite tools to motivate organizations to embrace and implement changes throughout the ages. I can't imagine embarking on a mission to change and improve culture without some kind of inherent motivation for those involved. It could be as simple as survival, or as complicated as world peace. Nonetheless, there must be, as I said above, a benefit derived by the participants. We were in a unique position, due to the autonomy permitted by voestalpine management, which I mentioned earlier in this book, to develop and implement a gain-sharing bonus explained below.

At the point that I initiated this "turnaround" and implemented this program, it was immediately apparent that (a) scrap and (b) supplies needed to be reduced, while (c) quality of product and (d) profit both needed to be improved.

Any time the company's performance improved over the established goal for each of those four elements above, more money was able to enter the bonus pool. The contribution to the bonus pool increased exponentially the greater our improvements over our goals. The process, in short, was this: Take company financial numbers by month, apply an algorithm that measures improvement and allow the algorithm to determine the bonus pool based on levels of success. The bonus was tracked, posted, publicly known and it was paid quarterly. On an annual basis, this bonus was equivalent to 10 to 15 percent of total compensation for the average employee.

It became apparent through the implementation of these programs that many of the company's first line leaders were not trained to lead CI initiatives. As a result, I developed a "Leadership Academy" for all company leaders. The program was based on the 12 basic leadership principles I determined were necessary to lead CI in our company. One of the 12 subjects was explored in a workshop offered twice every month, and each candidate was mentored by a member of the senior staff (who was charged with reinforcing the principles learned, discussing career development and helping their protégé solve their first problems). The program took one year to complete. The Academy was so successful that we created a "Team-Building Academy" for key non-leader positions (for instance, engineers and technical support) with a focus on conflict management, which exists in all strong and progressive teams.

Outside of leadership and team building, you will still continue to discover how important training is to continued success and sustainability within a continuous improvement culture. In addition to the leadership and team-building training we developed, my management team and I developed a "pay for skills" training development program for key skilled and unskilled positions in the company.

One last comment about training in a manufacturing environment: It's the most important thing we do — and the worst thing we do. But many people ask me: "How can I afford to do so much training?" The sincere answer I give: "We can't afford not to." Successful CI proves that your most valuable asset is your people, and therefore training is one of the best investments you can make.

> **Successful CI proves that your most valuable asset is your people, and therefore training is one of the best investments you can make.**

Allow me to restate several key rules to creating a successful CI culture:

1. **Management must lead by example.** Continuous improvement culture must be a top priority — and to make it one, your people must *perceive* it as one of your top priorities.

2. **Employees must have ownership.** This is the importance of a gain-sharing program like the one I just discussed. If you're not

prepared to share the success in such a way that it also benefits your employees, don't start. You'll be wasting your time.

3. **Tools are ultimately very simple.** Keep it all at a sixth-grade level. You want people focusing their energy on improving their work, not on figuring out complicated forms. This will be a continual challenge for you, since many of the issues you will encounter will not be simple problems. (*Keep reading for a rich set of resources on Lean Tools in Section II.*)

4. **Training is important.** It's the most important thing we do and, for most companies, it's the thing we do the worst. Be open to and continually invest in training for your people.

5. **Theme matters.** Give your program a name.

6. **Remember to sustain the journey.** You must evaluate the effectiveness of the whole program, and ask how it, too, can be improved. This should be done regularly — annually, at a minimum.

7. **Make CI a priority in your company, second only to safety and quality.** If you do that, profitability will come. If you do not have a designated leader of the CI initiative in your organization, hire or empower one today.

8. **Everyone participates.** It's a condition of employment, period. There should be zero tolerance for people who don't "buy in" to the concept. You will be surprised when some people (like production workers or professional managers) refuse to join the club. But as I like to say, "We provide them the opportunity to pursue their careers elsewhere." And that's the way it has to be.

This was, of course, a very basic approach to launching a CI culture. It met most of the standards and keys and rules that I've seen for successful programs. And it generated great results.

Wondering about the benefits my company achieved through its Continuous Improvement program, and which might also be possible in yours? Here are just a few of our accomplishments. We:

- Doubled value-added through increased efficiencies.

- Increased sales volumes, and maintained better customer and supplier relationships (they were even welcome at our internal improvement activities!).

- Maximized team member ownership (largely through gain sharing); employees ran a Lean company, avoided over-hiring and kept each other accountable.

- Better cost control and technology development — because everybody benefits from profitability.

- Developed stronger management/workforce relationships, and a clearer focus on accountability in a progressive atmosphere.

A successful CI culture — for any organization and any leader — is a choice. I'm endlessly grateful that I chose to pursue a CI culture and stick to its tenets, daily, even when doing so meant extra effort. The investments in the processes and principles, which always came down to being invested in our people, were a no-brainer. Our success as a company was tied to our continuous improvement culture. Your success can be equally guaranteed.

Chapter 11
Overview of Waste

Waste exists in every system. From manufacturing and assembly to hospitality, healthcare, transportation and social services, there's no escaping it. But there's plenty we can do about it.

Waste is a problem for businesses. Waste can cost companies millions of dollars at a time in some industries, and can wreak havoc on your bottom line in any field if you don't monitor it and take steps to minimize it. Especially for organizations that use Lean processes, eliminating waste is often one of the key elements of a continuous improvement program for this reason.

In specific terms, what waste does is increase costs to the "supplier," or your company, while adding no value to the end consumer. In short, waste is avoidable, needless loss that provides zero benefit. You knew that — but now you feel the responsibility to be rid of it!

> Waste is not just a loss, but avoidable, needless loss that provides zero benefit.

Waste also extends the period of Return on Investment (ROI), which means that the company's income (and capacity to continuously improve itself) is watered down. The engine cannot reach its full horsepower because someone put water in the gas. Like a deprived engine, wasteful companies' employees are frequently less engaged, and in some cases their energy for work can be skunked by wasteful processes — thus making the problem epidemic and systemic!

> **"The most dangerous kind of waste is the waste we do not recognize."**
>
> — *Shigeo Shingo*

Waste is defined into seven basic categories:

1. Overproduction

2. Defects & Rework

3. Motion/Transportation

4. Inventory

5. Over-Processing

6. Waiting

7. Underutilized Human Capital

These are also *hidden wastes*. If you'll notice, you can't precisely measure "waste" in any of the above categories — and in some cases, you wouldn't even notice the wastes if they weren't pointed out to you. That's why they're called "hidden wastes." It's no accident that Lean, waste-free companies seem overly disciplined and "vigilant" on the inside. They are attempting to be rigid in process compliance so that variation (waste) appears obvious.

OVERPRODUCTION

Overproduction waste occurs when a company manufactures, assembles or builds more than what is needed. It is the most dangerous of waste as it has a logarithmic impact on all the others. We make something just-in-case instead of Just-In-Time (JIT). *(By the way, see Section II of this book for an entire chapter on JIT.)* What leads to longer production runs? Inaccurate scheduling, long lead times, long changeovers and not being close enough to our customers to understand their changing needs. We worry that our customer might need more, so we choose to suffer with the associated cost of unsold goods and services. Overproduction is a trap; it appears to be a solution to the unchecked fear of unstable capability.

What to Look for: Processes producing more than what's being "pulled" by the customer. A red flag, if batching or storage is required during or between processes.

How to Reduce: Improve changeover and set-up times, and balance production.

DEFECTS & REWORK

Defect/rework waste occurs when a company doesn't have robust preventative systems that include Poka-Yoke and Mistake Proofing techniques. *(Again, read on! There's an entire chapter on Mistake Proofing in Section II.)* When we cause an error or defect and pass it on to the next operation — or worse, we pass it on to the customer — we are accepting rework as part of that process. We lose money when something is manufactured, assembled or serviced twice when our customer only paid once. Rework is the quintessential stupid tax — it eats margin across all four manufacturing disciplines: man, method, material and machine.

What to Look for: Defective, partial, or uncompleted products or services, and completed units that are reworked or thrown away.

How to Reduce: Improve Visual Controls and initiate more complete Standard Operation Procedures. Implement Mistake Proofing or Poka-Yokes at the source or the place errors occur. (Again, more details will follow in Section II as we "zoom in" on a lot of these techniques and tools.)

MOTION/TRANSPORTATION

Motion and Transportation waste is the unnecessary movement of people, product or equipment that adds no value to a process. Workers walk back and forth from the work area around unneeded equipment, or otherwise perform redundant motions that can be eliminated to speed up a process — and believe me, the time you'd save adds up much quicker than you'd think in many of these cases!

This can be one of the most frustrating wastes for workers and management — because it is physical — and it is obvious to the value adders who may not be empowered to change logistics. The lost time and production rob most processes of opportunities to function efficiently, and motion waste makes employees work harder. While most processes are not designed to have motion waste in them, it is one of the first wastes to "creep in" and cause disruption.

What to Look for: Excessive walking, moving or handling. Prepare a simple, but real, (spaghetti) diagram of the actual process flow. Ask the value adders, how can we make this simpler or easier for you?

MENTAL NOTE

A spaghetti diagram is easy-peasy; don't make it hard, don't try to make it perfect — just study the movement flow. Print or pencil draw a blank layout of the area, with block placeholders for capital equipment, buildings or process monuments, and then follow the value adder through their process steps. A second observer can time the process cycles and total time. A third observer can document word descriptions of the activities to further identify waste. In the end, your diagram may look like spaghetti traveling across the paper — this to visually identify travel patterns and redundant non-value adding waste.

How to Reduce: Develop and then examine a Value Stream Map and/or Physical Flow Map of every process and value-adding operator, equipment or material movement. *(Rest assured ... there's an entire chapter on Value Stream Mapping in Section II!)* Minimize the physical distance between materials and their users.

INVENTORY

Inventory waste hides many unwanted conditions. Excessive inventory may cover up quality problems, like rework and defects, manpower and/or production scheduling problems, excessive lead times, and supplier or vendor problems. It is very expensive to carry excessive inventory that requires capital to be tied up in interest payments (not to mention the original cost of the unneeded material). Again, excessive inventory depresses your ROI.

What to Look for: Excessive service capability and/or excessive inventory of raw materials or finished goods with less than 10 turn-overs per year.

How to Reduce: Implement Just-in-Time (JIT) movement of materials and kanbans. *(Yes, you guessed it! There's a chapter on kanbans in Section II. I've got you covered!)*

OVER-PROCESSING

Over-processing waste occurs when a company makes a product (or performs a service) better than a customer needs or is willing to pay for. Features that do not add value in the eye of the customer do not improve a product or process; in fact, they may harm the process. Not closely monitoring how customers use our products or services leads us to build in or provide features that we think they want or need. It is also caused by not having job standards and end user fit, form and function — Standard Operating Procedures (SOP) or over-engineering quality tolerance.

What to Look for: Products being returned without a clearly defined defect and corrective actions that repeatedly focus on 'retraining.' Fiscal profit margins eroding and processing cost, time and supplies increasing. Too much physical inventory. Work in progress (WIP) between processes, resulting in production line unbalancing — starts and stops — long and short production cycles chained together.

How to Reduce: Determine if the feature, service, or product is needed or costs more than customers will pay, given an extensive understanding of how customers actually use the service or product.

WAITING

Waiting waste comes from people, processes, or partially finished goods sitting idle while waiting for instructions, information or raw materials. Poor scheduling, poor vendor support or communications, and inaccurate inventories (causing you to fall short of items you need) cause processes and people to come to a halt and cost valuable time (and thereby profit).

What to Look for: Idle people or machines waiting on preceding operations, materials, schedules or information.

How to Reduce: Balance scheduled workloads and use a Cycle Time/ Takt Time Bar Chart for process synchronization (a takt time bar chart is a visual data collection tool used to reveal time imbalances within a value stream).

Note: The total manufacturing lead time or comprehensive value stream is the sum of individual cycles or processes within a process chain. It is nearly impossible to identify which aspect of the process made your shipment late, without analyzing the individual cycles within the chain. By timing individual process steps that exceed the takt calculation, bottleneck cycles are revealed. Undisciplined processes or cycles greater than takt guarantee imbedded waste (reduced employee morale, waiting/idle processes, inventory build-up between processes, expediting fees, overtime, late shipments, etc.), not to mention disappointed customers.

UNDERUTILIZED HUMAN CAPITAL

What is human capital? The extraordinary and infinite storehouse of your collective team members' expertise, customs, social behaviors and personas, natural intellectual capacity, physical fitness and educational expertise, personified or measured by its vast ability to yield economic value within a social construct (i.e., your business). Humans are the best part of your day and the worst part of your day.

American educator and author, businessman and speaker Stephen Covey, understood the monumental impact of authentically engaging human capital and the tragically wasteful result associated with underutilizing human capital.

> "At some time in your life, you probably had someone believe in you when you didn't believe in yourself ... Treat a man as he is and he will remain as he is. Treat a man as he can and should be and he will become as he can and should be."
>
> — *Stephen Covey,* The 7 Habits of Highly Effective People

This is a titanic topic — one that can sink or fortify your ship. When onboarding employees, figure out what values and methods you will systematize, then do it repeatedly well. It is critically important to get the right people inside your organization — especially if they coach or mentor other people. *Do not hire people to coach other people if those people don't like people.*

On the daily battlefield of business, you are perpetually calibrating and coaching the 4Ms to handle crisis. Crisis is the one constant. The 4Ms — *man, method, machine and material* — are your four resources of defect or waste entry. Of these four resources, the wo-man (both genders respected equally), is the most precious and the most complex. Humans are the quarterbacks of problem solving. Humans are the only intentionally dynamic (not static) capital in your business. In a stable business system, you want machines, materials and methods to remain fixed for repeatable results and predictive capability. Manufacturing is slave to process variation; you cannot improve that which cannot be repeated. Therefore, it is worth repeating the obvious: humans are not static capital, nor would you want them to be. Static things cannot think, problem-solve, create or evolve.

> **Humans are the quarterbacks of problem solving. Humans are the only intentionally dynamic (not static) capital in your business.**

Sheep Fable: I have worked with some organizations, where senior managers were rewarded for treating team members like sheep. We have all been trapped on the 'inside' of sheep nation. Most new people will try to stand up and behave like a shepherd, soon to be shoved down by other well-intended sheep or by the most frightened shepherds. Eventually, even the most talented employees don the sheep's skin or decide to leave the herd in the night. If they remain, with any dream of becoming a shepherd, or remain, secretly hurt from witnessing sheep colleagues turned lamb chop, they may begin to act like wolves and nibble on sheep nation. The shepherd who treats employees like sheep gets eaten by internal employees in sheepskins or the entire field gets eaten by murdering packs of wolves from outside sheep nation who have learned the value of working together as individuals.

It has been my experience that humans enjoy a steady introduction of structured and communicated change; variation feeds our natural desire for the new. Challenge keeps our brains and hearts interested, growing and inspired. Variation of experience increases our ability to successfully solve more difficult problems. The success of your intellectual capital to drink from a fire hydrant of change will be tested during a crisis. Limits will be discovered if too much change is introduced without absorption time and training. It is at this intersection when leaders must coach and encourage human capital to dig deeper, to work together beyond the crisis, to *engage hearts and minds to improve the company together.*

When your organizational culture genuinely values people more than any other capital resource, people rise to the vision of your expectation and faith in them, and remarkable results ensue.

What to Look for: Sheep nation — leaders of others, who see themselves as managers, not coaches or mentors. Employees refusing to think, a lack of ideation or sustained problem solving. A dividing wall between resource holders and value adders. Siloes in department discipline and/or teams. Repeating issues or quality defects that go unresolved. Negative or low work morale, to include hostility in the work place, high safety incident ratios and low attendance at company functions.

How to Reduce: Establish and proof hiring standards, values and processes, hire the right people, weed people out of coaching roles who do not work well with others, establish a culture of expectation and personal accountability. Expect your employee to think; when they make mistakes, prove to them that they are valued above other forms of capital and invest again.

You have now completed Section I of *Shut Up, Get Lean*. Are you ready to take the lessons of Section I to drive new thinking and managerial operations, and then open your mind to the use of several helpful tools that are outlined in Section II? Great! Keep reading.

SECTION 2

GETTING LEAN

Tools, Systems and Strategies You Can Use

Lean Assessments

To get started on your "getting Lean" process, you will need (among other things) an open and objective assessment that evaluates current practices on the shop floor. You need an insight into where production waste exists and how to remove it. The assessment should be simple enough for the shop floor personnel to use and have enough detail for management to know where to put the improvement efforts. A good assessment will reduce the cost of false starts during implementation and identify where the greatest ROI can be gained. Study your profit margins; where there is erosion, there is waste. It is always a good idea to involve Process Engineering and Fiduciary Accounting if possible — it goes without saying, ask the value adders, they know where money is being lost. If all else fails, take your forklift drivers, water spiders and/or logistics folks to lunch; they will spill the waste beans. They see it long before anyone else does.

An assessment of the entire organization should also include those non-manufacturing activities that influence the overall performance of the organization, including sales, order processing, purchasing and customer service. Wastes exist in each of these departments, I assure you — just as it does in manufacturing or assembly.

The assessment should be completed by more than one person, and a cross-functional team usually works best. Be sure to include someone from outside the work-center being assessed. Consultants or quality personnel from sister plants or associated organizations also provide a good source of "unbiased eyes."

When people working within a process assess themselves, they often cannot see the forest because of the trees. They are too close to the process and have become used to the way things are. But someone from outside the process who asks "Why?" will often lead to the discussion that reveals hidden waste and root causes.

The assessment should be designed to only identify potential improvement opportunities and estimate their impact on production. The assessment should not aim to identify how to fix the problems found or the assessment effort will die before it can begin. Focus on ROI and what success will look and feel like. Establish value-adder interest and participation first, or the assessment could be perceived as punitive or personally critical.

ASSESSMENT QUESTIONS

1. Have job instructions (Standard Operating Procedures) been standardized and are they being followed?

2. Are clear and easy-to-understand Visual Controls available to help the workers?

3. Are systematic replenishment practices being used to minimize temporary materials storage and transportation?

4. Are standardized containers and markings used as part of a materials scheduling and tracking system?

5. Are traveling or movement sequences for processes laid out to provide economical flow from beginning to end?

6. Are all tools properly accounted for at the end of each shift and do they have clearly marked and clearly designated homes? A fun question to ask is, where does this tool sleep when not in use?

7. Are SPC (statistical process control) charts being used on equipment to monitor effectiveness daily?

Your assessment will probably reveal the need to fix some things. And that's a *good* thing! What follows this chapter are detailed discussions of 11 Lean Tools you can use as you address the opportunities revealed by your assessment.

You may find that you need more than one of the tools. That's perfectly fine, normal even. Many of the tools can be used together as parts of a broader overall initiative because many of them complement one another.

These tools can be added to Six Sigma techniques to create a more dynamic improvement effort. Each tool will help to remove waste and reduce the cost of operations. No matter which tool you choose to start with, they can all save your organization money and eliminate waste.

6S

WORKPLACE ORGANIZATION USING THE 6S SYSTEM

1. **Sort** – Remove unneeded items

2. **Set in Order** – Identify "homes" for everything

3. **Shine** – Clean enough for inspection

4. **Standardize** – Create SOPs and instructions

5. **Sustain** – Support and reward

6. *SAFETY – A framework of thought around all 6S activity*

The 6S System is a workplace organization method that greatly improves the efficiency and management of an operational area while improving morale and saving time. The system hinges on five main tenets — sorting, setting in order, shining, standardizing and sustaining. And throughout those five steps should be an unflagging dedication to safety — the sixth S.

Because 5S (or 6S, as I like to call it because of the importance of safety) is often the first step in a company's application of Lean techniques, it helps to get all the "junk" out of the work area and then set procedures to keep it that way.

STEP 1: SORT

"Sort" means to go through a work area and remove all of the unneeded items. Workers and managers, left to their natural devices, have a habit of leaving items around that are no longer needed to perform the task. This results in unneeded clutter or obstacles in a work area. Removing these unneeded items and cleaning up the work area improves morale and safety.

> **Workers and managers, left to their natural devices, have a habit of leaving items around that are no longer needed to perform the task.**

An organization can have a "Red Tag" event that helps everyone buy into the idea that things are going to change in their work areas. Everyone gets involved in sorting through his or her area and identifying things to be removed permanently, removed to a better holding area or things that need to stay (and *must* have an identified "home," but more on that later). Be careful not to remove items that people are emotionally attached to without their agreement. 6S can be an emotional exercise for long-term employees, and an emotional tinder box in a low-trust culture. Process owners are of greatest concern when implementing 6S — you are in their sandbox.

Clearly mark the Red Tag Holding Area and monitor it closely. After 30 days, any remaining items should be recycled, sold or discarded. I bet you won't miss anything you get rid of at that point. Return needed items to the stock room, tool room, or wherever they should be logically inventoried.

This activity should include all administrative offices and support centers.

Look for items that are dusty or hidden behind or above other things. These items might include out-of-date materials, old instructions, broken or unused tools or tooling, unused computer or support equipment, old drawings, drawers that hide "junk," and miscellaneous extras and equipment. Don't forget to apply 6S disciplines to virtual storage space and virtual libraries — our newest challenge in today's demand for processing speed, cost reduction and data security.

> ### MENTAL NOTE
> Consider dedicating a controlled and manifested Red Tag Holding Area in every business location. Have fun with it; call it your Junk Yard Dog House or Yard Sale Library. Some companies with multiple locations have launched virtual Red Tag Holding Areas and put them online, so everyone can recycle and find new cost-effective uses for capital items, tools and supplies.

STEP 2: SET IN ORDER

"Set in Order" means to establish and mark a "home" for all of the needed items in a workplace. If there is a multi-shift operation, workers from the different shifts will leave tools, technical manuals and parts lying in different places after they use them. To improve processes and reduce cycle times, it is imperative to keep the needed items in designated places. "A place for everything and everything in its place" is the key to minimizing needless hunting for needed items, and therefore minimizing wasted time.

"A place for everything and everything in its place"
is the key to minimizing needless hunting for needed
items, and therefore minimizing wasted time.

One of the areas most improved by the 6S system is the supply or material stock area. From office supplies to chemicals to hand tools to safety equipment to cleaning materials, all resources should have designated homes. When you look at storage space for anything, you should be able to tell what item and how much of it belongs there.

Use shadow boards to identify misplaced or lost tools and small items. Paint markings on the floor where larger items are to be kept. Workers and management alike will have an easier time keeping track of everything, and the stress of chasing after misplaced or lost items will be greatly reduced.

Look for clearly marked and designated homes for all items (or, rather, places where you can establish those homes). Nothing should just be "lying around." Raw materials, work in progress and finished goods should all have designated homes.

Improve by designating homes for everything left from Sort (that is, everything not removed by the previous step in the process). Get the workers and managers involved in cleaning their own areas. Assign the task of developing a standard policy for the marking of similar items, like tools and support equipment. Set a standard for stripe size and color, labels and fonts, and specified colors for the homes of quality, safety and production items.

Often it is best to start with one area within the facility. Completely mark the area for all items to remain there. Use this area as an example for the rest of the facility. Don't forget maintenance, support and administrative areas. If there are multiple shifts or crews using the same areas, get representation from all groups to help in the activity of designating new homes for everything. Development of good Visual Controls can greatly enhance your 6S program. Everyone needs to work together, and management's support and involvement needs to be visible. This is the power of Visual Management — it is intuitive.

STEP 3: SHINE

"Shine" means to clean equipment and work areas well enough for an inspection. The best way to identify leaking hoses, loose connectors, scratched surfaces or damaged equipment is to clean them thoroughly. This cleaning process at the beginning and/or end of a shift provides immediate identification of potential problems that may interrupt services or even shut down entire facilities. Calibration markings, machine settings and lubrication points should be kept clean and their markings or labels easy to read. Work machinery and designated homes that are worn off should be repainted. Safety, quality and production signs should be clean and readable. Indications of early deterioration of equipment — like leaking seals, noisy motors, or excessive vibration — should be reported for repair as soon as possible. Checklists should be established to cover all the cleaning and inspection items. This will help everyone involved to understand and comply with the new requirements.

Look for old oil leaks that have spread to the floor or have covered up the exact leaking point. Identify areas that have not been cleaned for a long while because of the difficult location or lack of requirement. Take note of slippery floors, torn safety curtains, cracked hoses and greasy fingerprints on doors or covers of equipment.

> Everyone needs to understand why changes of habit are needed.

Improve by getting operators, maintenance personnel and managers to develop checklists that all can support. Everyone needs to understand why changes of habit are needed. Make the checklist easy to read and easy to use. The person doing the cleaning and his or her manager or team should both sign off the checklist after completion. Designated times for the cleaning and inspection should be established for each shift or crew. Management needs to ensure this cleaning and inspection becomes part of the daily routine and does not require overtime or is designated to be done in addition to their normal job. The checklist can have the details of items to be done and a photo with exact locations identified on one side and the sign-off roster with dates, times, signatures and a list of defects found on the other side. These checklists should remain with the equipment to be reviewed periodically for accuracy and correction of defects identified. Some organizations fill in the unneeded portions with grey and require check marks in the blank squares only when defects or problems are found. This provides an easy-to-read checklist and highlights problems more clearly. These checklists should help to speed up the improvement of undesirable workplace and equipment cleaning habits.

MENTAL NOTE

Shining is way more than "cleaning" — it is inspecting for the safety of the human and the machine.

STEP 4: STANDARDIZE

"Standardize" means to develop a checklist that everyone can understand and use. Develop expected standards for equipment and workplace cleanliness and let everyone know how important this cleanliness is to the success of the organization. Workers should use the checklist and take ownership by signing it. Management should review the checklist for compliance.

> **From the boardroom to the janitor's closet, 6S needs to become a cultural norm to be truly successful.**

Standardization requires management to get involved and lead the movement to make 6S work within your organization. Training must be provided for everyone to understand the new standards and requirements. Compliance to the 6S requirements should become part of the appraisal review process to emphasize its importance. From the boardroom to the janitor's closet, 6S needs to become a cultural norm to be truly successful.

STEP 5: SUSTAIN

In order to "Sustain" 6S, management and workers will have to work together to support and reward those who comply with these standard directives. Everyone should be able to see how they benefit from 6S and how it makes the workplace safer. Sustaining 6S for the long haul requires that middle managers and team leaders constantly monitor the worker's compliance. They must identify machines and work areas that are becoming worn and need repainting. Then management must schedule and complete the repainting to show everyone that this is not a one-time exercise and that 6S is an ongoing program.

> **Everyone should be able to see how they benefit from 6S and how it makes the workplace safer.**

Periodically updating locker rooms and dining areas and applying a 6S checklist to these areas will gain the attention of the workers and show them that all areas, including non-production areas, can be improved for everyone's benefit.

THE 6TH S: SAFETY

It is commonly accepted that President Theodore Roosevelt was the originator of the sentiment, "People won't care how much you know until they know how much you care."

Let me just get country-fried Kentucky honest on you. If you are stupid enough to launch a 6S campaign with your employees and don't make SAFETY a fundamental element of the program, you should be deep-fried.

Seriously, consider how to market all six of the elements of 6S before starting your campaign, and make the SAFETY element one that you blend into each of the preceding five areas of focus. Words are powerful, but actions eliminate the need for many words.

> Words are powerful, but actions eliminate
> the need for many words.

Do not tell your employees and customers that you value safety if your company is in fact dark, dirty and dangerous. It is time to walk the fields of production (gemba — go see where the value is added) and audit reality. 6S ... sometimes called Visual Factory ... is absolutely the foundation of your safety program. You cannot expect people to work safely in a dirty, disorganized and disordered space. Further, what is physically experienced is what your silent culture screams about your unspoken values. Picture the county carnival; now picture Disney World. You will know immediately what is valued.

According to the National Safety Council[1], every seven seconds, an American worker is injured on the job. And the top three workplace injury events resulting in lost work days? Overexertion (34 percent), contact with objects and equipment (25 percent), and slips, trips and falls (25 percent).

Employee safety is ultimately the employer's responsibility. There is absolutely no greater value than the establishment of a symbiotic relationship between work and organization. Well-meaning employees and even a few managers may ask, "Boss, you want me to clean or to make parts?" Your response must be an enthusiastic, "Yes!" They are two mutually beneficial efforts in cooperative relationship; together they increase efficiency, and apart they decrease efficiency. If your employees are not seeing these two efforts as one value, you have some cultural work to do.

6S: HOW TO MAKE IT STICK

No matter how many S's a company commits to, it still must instill a culture that allows the methodology to thrive. These tips can help accomplish that:

1. **Company leadership must provide visible support, not just lip service.** Employees can tell the difference between a corporate vision and just another activity thrown down from the front office. If they aren't sold on the value of an idea, employees won't participate in a meaningful way. I'm proud to say that when it came to RFC's company culture, goals and objectives, our people could see the focus. They saw that safety, Lean and continuous improvement were strategic initiatives for the success and well-being of the company and its employees. Truly, you will

---

1   https://www.nsc.org/work-safety/tools-resources/infographics/workplace-injuries and https://injuryfacts.nsc.org

engage hands and hearts when efforts materialize in gain sharing. Effort and reward *must* link.

> **Employees can tell the difference between a corporate vision and just another activity thrown down from the front office.**

2. **Educate everyone.** Don't just run through a slideshow. You've got to engage employees in kaizen events. You've got to involve value adders and let them make the changes. You might have a lead champion or a continuous improvement leader of the factory, but if that person is driving the initiative alone, it won't sustain itself. Your organization must become a teaching culture, one that intentionally cultivates combat multipliers — your sticking success is in the making of lieutenant leaders who motivate, develop and train up the next generation of champions.

3. **Be repetitious, revisit step 2 and continually educate everyone.** A company can't have one event and expect a culture to develop. The kaizen events — focused exercises to improve a specific process — pull the workers in, and continually holding these events reminds employees that the elimination of waste is a condition of employment, not just an exercise.

4. **6S Steps are Progressive and Must Be Established and Sustained in Order.** There is an advancing logic of application built into the order of the 6S Steps. You must SORT and maintain a commitment to that first step before you progress to SET IN ORDER ... and so on. A good way to teach the importance of this intentional progression is to suggest a spring clean out of your garage. You are not going to SET IN ORDER everything in your garage without first SORTING it. You get the logic — if there is backsliding and an erosion of a more basic step, advanced steps will appear too difficult to implement.

If everyone is involved, if everyone is hearing the same message and if those people have been involved in kaizen, good change rapid improvement events, you will get results within the course of a year. People want to be on a winning team; if you are disciplined in your preparation, coaching, mentoring and refining of technique every day, it makes "go time" (audit or tour day with your customers) not just tolerable, but fulfilling.

You know you have arrived when you observe your most-recently hired employees stop to pick up scraps of paper waste while walking through the company. Another indication of cultural arrival is when everyone knows that 6S disciplines are a form of value-adding production and employees no longer ask, should I produce or clean up? They naturally value both activities.

Rapid Improvement Processes (Kaizen)

A Rapid Improvement Process — or kaizen (Japanese word for "good change"), as it is more commonly called — is an intense five-day event that results in immediate change and bottom-line results. For greatest impact and cultural change, it is suggested that you host multiple events across the fields of production; both production and support or corporate teams can and should host kaizen events. Some organizations host single- or half-day events — what is important is that improvement ideas are completed during the event. Leftover kaizen activities are like leftover sushi, they're just not as attractive the next day. The success of this tool lies within two groups:

1. The first group consists of the senior managers. Before the rapid improvement or kaizen event begins, senior managers must actively support this effort by selecting specific improvement projects, most likely from information developed during the Lean Assessment or during a senior management brainstorming session.

2. The second group consists of the hourly workers who make up the largest portion of the cross-functional team. They must be enthusiastic about this event and understand their responsibility to identify problems and implement solutions.

Usually, a facilitator from outside the process begins the event with training on the tools to be used; by the first afternoon, employees are diving into the process headfirst. Data is gathered from the process in question and the team takes its own measurements of the process performance to help the team get more current and accurate information. Team members brainstorm possible solutions and examine the feasibility of implementing them.

These events can apply a single Lean tool, like quick changeovers, kanbans, or JIT techniques *(each of these tools has a dedicated section in this book, so keep reading!)*, but many of them apply a combination of several tools for the largest impact. Once the team has identified the improvements it needs to make, it starts to physically move equipment, machines, parts, materials and work areas to achieve its goals. The results are run as trials to ensure compliance with standards as well as production and quality requirements. Standard Operating Procedures are developed and tested on the new processes as part of the event.

At the end of the week, the team presents its changes to senior management and the anticipated financial ROI is explained. These events are the easiest and fastest way to get bottom-line results. Remember, though, that they are extremely active events by their nature, and can therefore cause major disruption in the workplace if not supported by management and understood by everyone.

Further, the results will only be permanent if management consistently supports the documented changes and if everyone looks for ways to *continually improve* the process, rather than simply tolerating it as it is. Remember, this is part of the journey, and part of the point: We should never stop looking for improvement opportunities!

QUICK CHANGEOVERS

Many manufacturers believe in traditional "long runs" for manufacture because it is supposed to be more efficient to run a big batch than to run several shorter batches that include changeovers. But the manufacturers that are leading their industries have found that just the opposite is true.

If changeover times are drastically reduced and simplified, we can changeover more often and please more customers. Today's customers do not want to hear that they have to wait for long runs of "other" products before you will get around to making their product. Quicker changeovers on smaller and more flexible equipment makes it easier to please many customers while reducing the overall cost of holding large quantities of inventory that is waiting for production opportunity.

> Today's customers do not want to hear that they have to wait for long runs of "other" products before you will get around to making their product.

Traditionally, manufacturing companies have identified the approaching end of a long run and, when finished, turned off the equipment. Workers then started to clear the machine of old products and went to get the necessary equipment and tools to do the next changeover. Old dies and tooling were pulled out, new dies and tools were installed, and adjustments necessary to produce the new product were made. With the changeover complete, workers cleaned up and then started up the equipment to begin the new run.

Typically, in the organizations where I worked and led, this process took anywhere from 1.5 to 6 hours. The actual changeover of dies and tooling took only 30 minutes to an hour. What were we doing all the rest of the time? To answer this question, we have to record the actual changeover very carefully and separate the external activities from the internal ones.

Many of the activities described could have been done "externally," while the equipment was still producing the last pieces of the first run. Only "internal" activities are the ones that require "Power Off." All the other activities can be done before or after the actual change-over and do not require Power Off.

MENTAL NOTE

If you are getting a new heart during a heart transplant surgery, you want the medical team to have done some "external" preparation for your surgery, like picking up the donated heart at the airport (JIT) and warming it up in surgery with your previously donated blood. You certainly don't want them to put you to sleep ("shut you down"), saw into your sternum ("internal") and then inquire about the Uber that was supposed to get your heart at an unknown location.

The first step to drastically reducing total changeover time is to have as many changeover tasks performed "externally" as possible, while the end of the current run is still finishing with Power On. An additional person (or the operator who has the time, in many cases) can prepare by collecting the required dies and tooling, specifications and needed transfer equipment ready without shutting off the equipment or ending the first run.

The same is true after the dies and tooling are in and adjustments have been made: The equipment can be turned on to start producing new parts while the old dies, tooling, tools and transfer equipment are returned to their proper locations. These first improvement steps cost almost nothing to change, but are sometimes the hardest to do because of years of old habits and resistance to change.

Once many of the old "internal" activities have been moved to external and are done before or after Power Off, the next step is to reduce the time required for the remaining internal activities. A valuable resource available on the subject is *A Revolution in Manufacturing: The SMED System* by Shigeo Shingo. His referral to SMED stands for Single Minute Exchange of Dies. (He believes the target for all changeovers should be nine minutes or less. Pretty fast, huh?)

SMART APPROACHES TO REDUCING CHANGEOVER TIMES

There are many ways to reduce changeover times. Installing and removing dies or tooling can go faster with roller tables or conveyors. Often, transfer equipment can be modified to also serve as installation and removal devices. Hydraulic clamps can be used in the place of screws or bolts along with guide pins and hard stops for alignment. Connectors can be ganged together and hoses can be joined using a manifold to reduce the number of connections to take off and reconnect. Set screws that require specific tools and are used for tightening can be replaced with knobs and fasteners that can be tightened quickly by hand.

And, of course, the handling of dies, tooling, tools and spec sheets can be improved in most facilities. All the dies and tooling should have their status (i.e., serviceable, broken or being modified by engineering) clearly marked and tagged using visual control techniques. Likewise, all of the tools and the spec sheets should have specific homes that are clearly marked and should be returned to their homes after use. These 6S practices make the overall process of completing a changeover less stressful for everyone involved.

If you put together a cross-functional team from maintenance, operations, quality assurance and the tooling department (if it is separate from maintenance), the results can be amazing. These people have many ideas on how to improve changeovers and reduce the time required. They need to be empowered to suggest, plan and implement these improvements.

So now, we begin to see how all of these tools, together with people who "get it" (those who buy into the culture and improved way of conducting business), really do make a difference. In cases like these, it's the sum of all the little tools, and all the people using them, that can overturn the old idea that "long runs are better." There are many outdated and faulty ideas like this that a good organization can overturn.

SEQUENCING

Now let's talk a little about where you start to see these tools come together.

One of our big examples and role models is The Toyota Production System. Toyota revolutionized just-in-time (JIT) techniques by sequencing their manufacturing of automobiles for mixed model production. In other words, they learned how to get into an incredible rhythm when manufacturing cars (good cars) that were all different types, and without having big interruptions on the assembly lines.

Their implementation of Lean techniques allows them to effectively produce the correct model of automobile with any of the variations needed to meet changing customer demands. Similar models that require different parts are scheduled for production with the right parts delivered to the assembly points just in time. These techniques can be applied to any production line that (a) produces similar items and (b) knows the frequency of their customer demands.

There is no need to tell customers that they have to wait until you complete a long production run of one type of product before you can produce a similar product. Operations that are *process-focused* rather than *function-focused* — with smaller machines and well-trained operators, of course — are usually flexible enough to use sequencing.

MENTAL NOTE

Simply defined, sequencing means components and parts arrive at a production line right in time (as scheduled) before they get assembled. The system must be fully time and product balanced — it is an assembly ballet, with seamless flow.

If you know today that you need to produce 60 Type A items, 40 Type B items, 20 Type C items and 5 Type D items, which all have the same foundation or base assembly, you can apply sequencing for maximum efficiency. You can make that (or any other) arrangement of different goods on any given day without substantial slowdown or interruption. Quick changeovers make sequencing possible.

Historically, organizations might produce, say, 125 Type As in one day, then 125 Type Bs the next day, and so on until they meet the requirements for all types. Aside from creating more storage and logistical difficulty, this method keeps the customers for types C and D waiting for their goods. In today's market, customers don't want to wait for their product while your competition is producing goods when the customer wants it — just in time. Sequencing allows you to provide various similar products from one production line in the quantities needed daily.

Zoning and Cellular Layouts

A cellular layout of any value-adding aspect of your business should provide all the equipment, tools, work instructions and materials to accomplish a single task or group of related tasks. It does not matter if the cell shape is a T, I, L, U or V. The best shape is the one that produces the most efficient production in a safe manner. If cells are U or V shaped, they should first be set up to flow counter-clockwise because most people are right-handed, and this is therefore the most ergonomically correct way to move parts or objects.

> **The best cellular layout is one that produces the most efficient production in a safe manner.**

Arrange cells to minimize the stretching and reaching for parts, supplies or tools, and to accomplish tasks. Place the height of the work surface based on the type of work to be done and the weight of the materials to be moved. Observe, consult with and include the employees doing the task before determining final layout.

Zoning is a technique of identifying the boundaries of a particular work center. When kanbans and 6S are added to a cellular layout, materials flow into and out of the process area (zone) with ease. Everything has a marked home and there is no excess work-in-progress storage. See how the tools and techniques combine well?

> ## MENTAL NOTE
>
> Do not "pay stupid tax" by leaving value adders out of process change decisions; you are in their crib, house, sandbox, you are a guest. When you leave, nothing sustains unless you have sincere buy-in from the value process owner.

When JIT is fully implemented, equipment and personnel will be optimized in new layouts. Techniques like frontal loading, retrieval and ergonomically correct work centers should be implemented. Be sure, as examples, to place supply and removal paths at least one meter away from the backs of workers and establish the paths at least two meters wide to reduce possible accidents. Some organizations establish "parts supermarkets" to locate materials near where they will be needed and operators "pull" materials into their work center, versus having work "pushed" to them.

Just-In-Time (JIT)

Every one of our activities in life could be called a process. From simple tasks, like bathing and eating, to complex tasks, like designing and building rockets, the things we do are usually "work in progress" (WIP). When we examine our activities as processes — especially in the context of work — we usually want them to be efficient, reliable, safe, low-cost and done at the right time.

The speed of a process is usually measured in *cycle time*. The total time required to produce a product or service from start to finish is called manufacturing lead time (MLT), a sum of all the linked cycle times within a process value stream. Therefore, cycle time reduction can improve costs for our customers and us. That's the broader goal for right now — reducing the length of cycle times, and thus overall MLT.

One technique that can shorten cycle time is *Just-in-Time or JIT* practices. When you provide materials, services or people *just before* they are needed, right where they are needed, and in the proper arrangement and orientation, there is a reduction of waste in the process. When examining these processes, note that work in progress (WIP) in the form of raw materials or partially completed work should be kept to a minimum between processes and at the starting point of processes. If providing this WIP is included in the process cycle time, as it probably should be, providing excessive WIP or providing it before it is needed ultimately just extends the process cycle time.

When management accepts JIT as a method of doing all business and begins to implement it, most people fear the possibility of frequent, small-size deliveries. They are afraid they will run out of work to do and will be delayed in their production. A comprehensive JIT system considers that schedules for manpower, materials and machines must be balanced to meet customer needs, both when they need it and at the quality required. These requirements are for internal, as well as external, customers.

The Single Piece Flow technique allows us to only make the quantity needed to fill the hole or to be "pulled" by the next operation downstream from their operation. This keeps the WIP to a minimum and is usually managed with a good kanban system. *(More on kanbans later in this Section of the book, I promise!)*

Before you start to implement brand-new JIT techniques or change any floor layouts, you should study the current process thoroughly and document it with a flow chart or Value Stream Map.

A few other things to remember as you start JIT:

- Remember that employee training in the necessary processes and procedures will be vital to your success.

- Don't underestimate the possible cost of these changes. They may be costly. Think of them as the investment they are.

- Tools and equipment need to be flexible and available to the people who use them. Avoid building any new walls or barriers that impede the flow of work.

- The implementation team should be interdepartmental and from all levels of the organization. It needs to work on everyone's level.

- The implementation team will need to be creative and not be afraid to make mistakes. This is sometimes a tricky change to make.

Teams may come up with ideas for bells, whistles or lights to be signals for replenishment of materials just-in-time. It is suggested to make temporary devices as signals and let the workers within the process area try them and modify them to meet their needs (and the needs of the production schedule). This trial-and-error method helps to build buy-in from all concerned parties and often generates additional ideas that engineering or management personnel might not have had. Worker involvement in setting up the JIT system in their work area or zone is critical because they'll have good direct input, seeing as their work zones are where they will spend the most time and where they have true expertise.

Mistake Proofing (Poka-Yoke)

At one time or another, we have all put something together upside down or backwards and still have it fit. But then, it probably didn't work as advertised when we turned it on or used it. Can someone do something the wrong way and still pass it on to the next step in your process?

Poka-Yoke is the method of applying Mistake Proofing techniques to eliminate the very possibility of many errors occurring. Workers, engineers and managers all must work together to write procedures and to design devices that prevent errors from occurring at their source of origin. Remember: *The best, most efficient, most cost-effective and safest place to catch errors is always at their source of origin.*

> **The best, most efficient, most cost-effective and safest place to catch errors is always at their source of origin.**

Inspections that discover errors but do not provide feedback after completion and have no chance of reducing defects (creating only wasted effort) are called *judgment inspections.* Inspections that provide data and information about where and when errors occur, and can be of assistance in preventing future errors, are called *informative inspections.* The inspections that identify, fix and/or prevent errors from happening at the point at which they could or do happen are called *source inspections*. The key issue here is that source inspections prevent errors from being passed on to the next step in the process and provide preventative and corrective action data. Source inspections are also known as in-process inspections within some organizations.

Source inspections check 100% of the processes or products that pass through one point of the operation or process. Source inspection devices can be switches, jigs or fixtures that halt the operation or stop the process if materials are provided upside-down or backward, if the wrong type or quantity of materials is provided, or if the machine or product is handled incorrectly. These source inspections should be a critical part of a comprehensive Zero-Defect program.

Often, bells, sirens or lights are used as signals that a source inspection has discovered a defect or error. These warning or control systems notify an operator of a problem and signal for the machine to be shut off, or accompany an automated shutdown of the equipment. These warning or control systems are usually attached to a *sensing device* that uses contact or motion methods to determine a problem exists. Contact methods include passive devices, such as guide pins, specially shaped or standardized fixtures, and jigs that will accept only one size or not operate if installed incorrectly. Limit switches and touch or antenna switches identify passage of a desired characteristic or object or the presence of an unwanted characteristic or condition. Energy-sensing devices and physical-contact devices can be used to sense motion, pressure or absence of an object.

While many different devices are available for all sorts of conditions to be monitored, one primary use is constant — they are used to detect errors or defects and prevent them from reaching the next operation or ultimately reaching the customer.

Value Stream Mapping

When we look at the entire process behind a product, we get the overhead view of a "value stream." We can break it up into each of its component pieces. Most processes start with a request for "action" or a product, and end only when the product or service has been delivered. Value Stream Mapping looks all the way from the finished product backward through the process to the raw materials or initial request for action. Now we can really see parts fitting together!

If your process is person-to-person, person-to-machine or machine-to-machine, Value Stream Mapping can help you to clearly understand — and therefore communicate — all the steps in a process. Value Stream Mapping also allows you to identify any hidden wastes that exist within a process. Often, hidden wastes are the largest cost of providing services or making products, so when you use Value Stream Mapping to identify the value added and non-value-added steps, the non-value-added steps within your process — which are waste — are highlighted.

From the raw materials storage to delivery of a finished product or service, materials flow throughout a process and are handled by many people and machines. Information also flows all the way from initial request for a product or service to the end, which is the customer's reception of the product or service. Most flow-charting or mapping processes do not include this crucial element called *information flow*. Value Stream Mapping not only includes information flow, but also shows how it is intertwined with material flow, machines and manpower.

> Value Stream Mapping not only includes information flow, but also shows how it is intertwined with material flow, machines and manpower.

An organization's information system is the communication link that holds together the manpower, machines and materials. Do not underestimate its importance.

Your Value Stream Map is first drawn in terms of its current process condition. This "Current State Map" identifies the process exactly as it exists today. Then, your Value Stream Mapping process will go on to identify a vision of how the process could be improved and is shown as such in a "Future State Map."

All the elements can usually be displayed on a single sheet of paper, which gives a comprehensive view of the entire process and provides a clearer understanding of how all the steps and wastes co-exist in the system.

Use symbols that are agreed upon and understood by the workers and management. Keep the symbols simple and draw them with a pencil before committing them to a computer or a complicated drawing. (It works best when each team member uses an 11-by-17 sheet of paper and draws a picture of how he or she sees the process first, just to get people thinking visually.)

Then, as a team, they can compare their drawings and discuss the accuracy of each. This usually requires a few trips back to the shop floor to verify the facts. Most processes are not laid out as we have them pictured in our minds. Even if you have to go back and check the facts, and even if the facts aren't pretty, draw it as it actually is. This exercise often reveals many hidden wastes and opportunities for improvement, and you won't see them unless you're open to seeing them.

Kanbans

If you need to change the way you schedule materials, including internal and external suppliers, kanbans may be the best tool to use. (Kanban is the Japanese word for signboard or signal board.) Traditional management systems like Manufacturing Resource Planning (MRP) may not support your plan to adopt Just-In-Time practices, lot size reductions or mixed-model production. Good preparation with standardized containers (for material movement) and physical tickets to signal needs and movement instructions will provide good support for the other tools and techniques you want to implement.

Basic kanban principles translate to some of the following techniques and applications:

- Empty containers accompanied by a ticket that says "fill me."

- Full containers staged with precise maximums clearly marked.

- Tickets displayed in the "make" area that cause precise quantities to be made.

- Tickets attached to full containers that cause product to be moved to defined destinations.

- Marked "floor parking spaces" or marked shelf space to limit overproduction.

- Maintaining a tight loop of ticket flow that minimizes opportunities for quality-related reworks.

- Housekeeping and safety practices that greatly assist kanban scheduling.

- All of the people involved knowing what's going with visual kanban scheduling.

Materials and production planners can use many of the same skills that they did in traditional environments. Instead of having to regularly feed elaborate planning systems or manually intervene in the production process, planning professionals use their skills to define, then redefine, the number of containers and tickets to be employed in particular processes. Same skills, but a much less tedious application.

In its simplest form, a planner's job is to determine the level of daily quantities (per part) and the desired standard container content. The daily demand number is divided by the standard container content number to determine the number of uniquely marked tickets that should be issued in the process. In some settings, set-up quantities or lengthy transportation routes cause planners to "fudge" the arithmetic to issue a few extra tickets.

Here's a specific example that applies kanban:

> In a factory with Visual Controls and proper JIT supplier agreements, plans are in place to make 600 assemblies every day during the peak season. According to the plans, 20 finished assemblies are to be nested in sturdy containers for movement to an adjacent department. Planners would therefore issue 30 make-and-move tickets, which would facilitate steady production. The "piece-parts" in this assembly example would likewise

be controlled with kanban techniques. Tickets would be used just the same during the assembly process.

In this example, to be even more specific, you could use a "two-bin" kanban approach, and that would also create an adequate visual signal. That is, parts from one bin would be consumed in production, at the production pace, and, when empty, the second bin is pulled into place and the first empty bin is placed in a signal station (parking space) that says, "fill me." The "fill" (replenishment) cycle must, of course, be shorter than the consumption cycle of the full bin.

Kanbans can facilitate very steady production using simple visual controls — as long as all production personnel commonly understand it. Together with other visual controls, they can have a huge, low-cost impact on production and efficiency.

Standard Operation Procedures (SOPs)

To ensure that your quality standards — in terms of consistency, effectiveness, efficiency, product quality and other quality measures — are realized, you are required to document the step-by-step process that defines how you need to do the work you need to do. An SOP (standard operation procedure) provides a baseline to answer the question: "How do we do that?" (It can also provide an answer to the sometimes-more-difficult question: "How *did* we do that?")

> By providing a stable, baseline process, SOPs make it easier to coach/instruct employees and control change for process improvement — which then makes continuous improvement possible and sustainable.

SOPs should be used wherever a work process is (or should be) documented. Verbal instructions change over time, from person to person, and are easy to forget. We provide a documented procedure as a baseline to ensure a stable, controlled work process. Good SOPs can be represented with pictures, words, tables, symbols, colors and visual indicators that communicate a consistent message to a diverse work group. By providing a stable, baseline process, SOPs make it easier to coach/instruct employees and control change for process improvement — which then makes continuous improvement possible and sustainable.

SOPs must be simple, user-friendly and helpful, not burdensome. Take inputs from all areas of the organization and collect information from everyone so that your SOP is most correct and helpful for everyone, and thus conducive to doing a job correctly the first time. Remember that the goal of an SOP is to document the best way to perform a job for your situation, materials, equipment, location and people. The SOP should be written specifically for you, the people using it and referring to it. This will help guarantee that you really are doing the work in the best way — at least until the next improvement comes along.

As a corollary to using SOPs, be sure your records and record management methods are up-to-date and that you properly safeguard all vital records. Vital records include any records that are difficult or impossible to replace and are essential to continued operation of the organization. SOPs and vital records should be near to one another because SOPs will help to fill gaps and describe day-to-day operations along with those vital records and recent data. They also provide a permanent record of procedure (and any changes to it), negating the unreliability of memory and verbal record. When it comes to managing the risk to the business, SOPs help to protect the business in crucial ways.

In any organization, the most difficult thing to impel is substantial change: change to people, change to products and services, changes to management systems, and even changes to whole organizations along Lean practices and principles. The complexity level of any change is significant, more than you initially expect, but SOPs give us simple tools to implement for gain and maintaining the gain.

SOP CHECKLIST

SOPs should be:

- Easy to read (be sure to take into account the language skills of your workers).

- Visually understandable (large, clear pictures or drawings).

- Inclusive of the provided tools and materials.

- Tested and approved by workers and management.

- In compliance with safety and quality standards.

MENTAL NOTE

The SOP Holy Grail is the Lego Puzzle example. Every picture delivers intuitive direction — it is a genius example to follow when creating SOPs. It is easy, stress free and pictorial.

Total Productive Maintenance (TPM)

A continuous improvement program can be enhanced with a *Total Productive Maintenance*, or TPM, program. TPM involves both the operators and the maintainers working together to improve the overall operation of the equipment. The operators are around the equipment all of the time and should be the first to identify noisy or vibrating motors, squeaky fan belts or chains, or oil and air leaks. Operators need to understand the basic standards for their equipment and check it closely every shift or day to ensure it meets those standards. As soon as a minor defect in operation is identified, maintenance needs to be notified. Catching problems early and fixing them is the key to preventing catastrophic failure or complete shutdown of expensive equipment.

Operators + Maintenance + Management = TPM Success

Maintainers need to work closely with the operators and educate them on what to look and listen for in order to have early detection of potential problems. A TPM system is owned by the operators, maintainers and management. Scheduling downtime for preventative maintenance, lubrication, cleaning and general inspections is key, and managers must ensure it happens. TPM and 5S/6S work hand-in-hand to provide a safer and more productive workplace and to dramatically reduce costly downtime.

Operators can be trained to make many repairs, such as the replacement of belts and/or hoses. They can learn how to add oil or lubricant when needed. The operators need to make the cultural shift to being the "owners" of their equipment and be held responsible for its upkeep. They need to see maintenance as a teammate.

Most failures occur when equipment is new or old. Lack of attention or proper upkeep will accelerate the aging process and shorten the life cycle of the equipment. Working together, operators and maintenance workers can extend the life of equipment and identify failures before they become serious and interrupt valuable production time. This team needs to include management as a strong supporter; operators and maintainers must have the confidence that management will schedule sufficient downtime for periodic and/or scheduled maintenance and will spend the money for needed repairs.

Development of an Overall Equipment Effectiveness (OEE) record can help to identify performance reduction before it becomes a total loss of performance. Most effectiveness reports monitor three key areas: equipment availability (time), equipment performance (speed) and quality of output.

The amount of time that a piece of equipment is not available because of minor stops, breakdowns, scheduled maintenance or because it's waiting for an operator is usually subtracted from the total time to give a percentage or rating of availability.

TPM can be included in a 5S/6S checklist or can be another checklist. When done together, it gets everyone involved and the responsibility is shared.

An OEE record should be displayed with a graph and be easy for everyone to document and understand. The operators should document the actual occurrences of downtime, no matter the cause or the length of time. When charted correctly over time, problems will repeat themselves and lost production trends can be identified and corrected.

SECTION 3

STAYING INSPIRED

Stories to Encourage and Guide You

CREATING INTENTIONAL VALUE IN AN UNINTENTIONAL WORLD

Value means something different to everyone. To a 16-year-old child, the value of a car means that the price of the car is equal to, or greater than, the number of hours they will have to work to make the payments. To me, safety features measure the value of her car. To others, it means benefit — does the car look aesthetically pleasing, have a great stereo system, get efficient gas mileage? Simply defined, value is the worth of something to a person — what someone is willing to pay for the item.

When you hear the phrase "value for money," it implies that the buyer is price sensitive. Other consumers reverse the phrase saying, "money for value" (meaning the buyer is willing to pay more for increased benefits, brand reputation, quality or more convenience, etc.).

When used in our everyday vernacular, the individual's definition of value is as unique as the customer's personal standard or experience. However, when vernacular becomes a technical business strategy — to Create Customer Value — the meaning of value must be precise, so that everyone creating value understands:

1. What Creating Value means.

2. How we measure it.

3. How we intentionally create more of it.

Creating Customer Value Means: We retain jobs and grow market share and reputation that advances our fiscal security. At the end of the day, we are all families working together to protect those that invest in us and in one another. It means the same thing to our paying customers.

How We Measure the Creation of Customer Value: If customers perceive the cost paid is less than the benefit received, value results. Therefore, the strongest measurement of Customer Value Creation may be perception. Are we better than all the other known choices? Are we easy to do business with, and do we really have smarter, safer, faster, quality solutions? Do our repeat customers become loyal partners? Do our customers tell others about our value? What do the market and our customers say about us? These are the measures of Customer Value.

> The strongest measurement of Customer Value Creation may be perception.

How do we intentionally create more Customer Value in an impersonal and unintentional marketplace, amid the quick and faceless rise of mass electronic media and colossal invisible suppliers that dominate consumers with cheaper products, like, Amazon, Walmart, etc.? Listening to and meeting the customer face-to-face, where they define value, seems more important today than ever. Set yourself apart from the competition by being intentional with your customer service, engineering processes, safety culture, quality discipline and continuous improvement efforts. Intentionality is your secret weapon and primary creator of more customer value.

Set yourself apart from the competition by being intentional with your customer service, engineering processes, safety culture, quality discipline and continuous improvement efforts. Intentionality is your secret weapon and primary creator of more customer value.

Value is created as much by focusing on internal culture as it is on processes and systems. You can't fake a culture of caring for the customer; they will know if it is sustainable. It is easier for competitors to copy products and systems than to emulate your long-standing culture of caring. Success lives in the mindset of your employees — the thoughts, hearts and words demonstrated in the intentional culture of employees. Yes, employee skills, systems and engineering solutions are critical, but the individual heart and the desire to create a positive customer experience are what ultimately create value for the buying customer.

The most important work we do every day is to understand our customer's need and perception of value. We all have real-life examples of value creators and value destroyers. I ask myself when I am with an employee or paying customer, "What can I do to create more value for my customer?" Am I asking the right questions, am I listening to them intentionally? Do they believe that I value the importance of our partnership; and value equally their sustained success? *Being intentional is never easy; it is the road less traveled and, yes, it makes all the difference.*

A Pay-It-Forward Habit

Organizational culture design is a fluid and complex topic. Our well-intended attempt to homogenize culture quickly puts us in a philosophical debate. Culture is not something that can be mass-produced or standardized. Its influence and power rest in the fact that it is unique and genuine to the system in which it serves.

Simply stated, organizational culture is the constellation of underlying values, beliefs, assumptions and ways of interacting that contribute to the unique social and psychological environment of an organization. This unseen "culture thing" is the defining characteristic of any social environment. A powerful ambiguous giant, culture inspires value propositions and drives human interactions at all levels of a social group. Like many "decisions in life," the truest measure of any action or culture is the value it yields.

Good cultures yield generations of employees who produce something of value — principle-based values (those that endure over time), empowered proactive decision-making, problem solving, progressive margins, visual factories, safe processes and a marketplace reputation of excellence.

Companies who practice the foundational habit known as Pay-it-Forward have significant success with the open display and engagement of this concept as a business value. What exactly is paying it forward?

The *Oxford English Dictionary* Defines It: To respond to a person's kindness to oneself by being kind to someone else.

Origin of the Pay-it-Forward Concept: First introduced in *Dyskolos*, an ancient Greek play in 317 B.C. The concept was rediscovered and described by Benjamin Franklin. The expression has been brought into popular culture by the bestselling novel, *Pay It Forward*, by Catherine Ryan Hyde, which was later adapted into a film of the same name.

On day one, a new employee enters a culture of gratitude or thanklessness that reinforces a resulting behavior. The habit or value of gratitude will quickly teach your new employee to pay-it-forward to others. If employees are empowered and expected to pay-it-forward, as demonstrated by leaders and mentors, it will reap dividends of value-adding behavior. At the core of a pay-it-forward culture lies the will to help people, to offer solutions to problems and make people's lives better.

Here are some examples of how reinforcing foundations of gratitude will pay-it-forward for years. Consider making it a key value.

- New hires receive 24 hours of mentor-guided orientation training.

- New hires immediately join CI teams dedicated to topics like Ideations, Cost Savings, or Voice.

- Annual Rallies – CI Teams are rewarded and recognized.

- Quarterly bonuses awarded to employees.

- Employees invited to volunteer in firefighters' services and non-profit organizations.

- Chamber of Commerce – membership and leadership.

- Area Technology School – engineering volunteers and internship programs.

Foundational Research: The Greater Good Science Center at the University of California Berkeley, which offers science-based insights for healthy living, has listed five ways Pay-It-Forward is good for you:

It promotes corporations and social connection.

- Giving is good for health.

- Giving makes us feel happy.

- It evokes gratitude.

- Giving is contagious.

Show Me the Money!

Simply put, executives have a responsibility to investigate the monetary impact of a continuous improvement project (CIP) on an organization. That means examining benefit-cost ratio, percentage of ROI, payback period and numerous other factors fully and accurately before reaching a conclusion; implementer confidence alone won't justify resource investment.

Return on investment (ROI) calculations are challenging; accurately isolating the effects of a program, converting the benefits to a monetary value, identifying the intangible benefits and calculating fully loaded costs will make even the most fastidious accountant break into cold sweats. Fortunately, information technology and real-time reporting capabilities have revolutionized the accuracy of ROI payback.

Today's global enterprise continues to expand in complexity. The speed at which information travels will continue to accelerate, requiring systems that are nimble and flexible. Small to mid-sized organizations, which often don't have dedicated teams for this kind of tracking, have little hope of responding effectively without applying a technology-based solution for tracking and assessing ROI.

Some companies undergoing continuous improvement processes have developed applications to track this kind of fiscally focused data, given all the inputs unique to their business or industry. A business's need for sustainability, scalability, history and standard project value costing have proven that, for some companies, it's worth the cost.

RFC's "Cost Saving Tracker" (an online software application idea library) has only begun to impact their continuous improvement culture. They have found that the Tracker's history files have become a virtual think-tank of ideas; because anyone in the company can browse the entries, it is common for team members to research the history files for benchmarking information. Intrinsically, entry visibility creates accountability and competition and encourages idea sharing. The Tracker itself has been an efficiency improvement tool for team members, eliminating subjective paper entries — but it's also a systematic way of saying, "show me the money!"

Broken Pots and the Art of Innovation

Imagine your organization as a huge, beautiful piece of pottery. It has taken you and your team years to painstakingly detail the clay, every last little inch. Each intricate detail tells its own story of collaboration, problem-solving and practical creativity. But, upon close inspection, you can find tiny cracks in the clay. Over time, the cracks widen into fractures and as more time passes, however slowly, the fractures spread. Left unchecked, the beautiful vase would break, but you attentively patch, retouch and repair however you can. But the deeper the cracks, the more delicate the repair and the more carefully your team finds itself tiptoeing around at work. You might find yourself simply trying to turn the blemished parts away from public view, toward the wall, so that no one looks at them.

Whatever form your organization's "cracks," when did they first appear? What caused them? Are cracks spreading and growing faster than innovation can fix them?

If there seems to be no innovation left in your organization, in the clay itself, then perhaps it's time to stop examining what's wrong with the vase and look instead at the potter. But this doesn't have to be a cause for discouragement; it may very well be an opportunity to "make a break" and change the company for the better.

On the topic of breaking pots, have a look at this photograph. That's an example of *kintsugi*, the Japanese art of fixing broken pottery with a gold-dusted lacquer resin. As a philosophy, it speaks to the breakage of pottery as a natural part of its history and something to be kept, not disguised. It implies that the pottery is actually more beautiful and rare for having had a history — for having had moments of breakage and repair. Like the owners of clay pots, if you intend to improve your company and create a better organizational balance, it's essential that you develop this attitude of valuing something "broken" as something still greatly worth owning and worth investing in. A company with cracks deserves, perhaps, the largest investment of gold to secure its future.

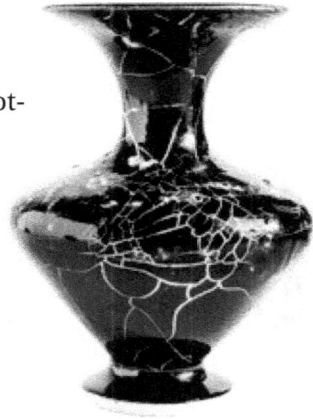

DIFFERENT MINDSETS, BETTER INNOVATION

When thinking of how you want to recast your new company culture, it's important to have a balance of engagement among your employees between the technical-minded (the "IQ" folks) and the "people" people (the "EQ" or "emotional [intelligence] quotient" folks). The balance of these forces within your company will largely determine your capacity to solve problems. In fact, without a good balance, your ability to innovate will be severely hindered. So let's talk a little more about the needs of each type of employee.

Technical (IQ) people have a high need for competence and correctness. When the senior architect, critical thinker, principal engineer or equivalent person gets something wrong, it stings on a personal level. That pressure (natural for that sort of person) can often cause that already-exacting personality to clamp down on eliminating inconsistencies or lapses. But a certain amount of "sight" is lost on these people when this happens; they miss other details. Left only to these devices, the proverbial pots will start cracking.

Empathetic (EQ) people have a high need for reflection and self-awareness and have a need to extend those attributes to the group or organization as a whole. Their understanding of the "human element" of situations is a potentially powerful resource, but their focus on relationships can cause accuracy and quality to slip. Left to their own devices, these people too will cause the pots to begin to crack.

We can see how the two types of people need one another! Probably you've already placed yourself as one sort of person or another (and maybe silently judged the other), but you can see how they offset one another's shortcomings. A good balance of these types is essential for an environment of innovation. A culture of innovation cannot be manufactured, but is rather the byproduct of a work environment that cultivates employee autonomy, mastery and purpose.

> If you ever hear employees say, "That's an old problem; we'll never fix it," you're hearing the voice of a culture that prefers known failure to unknown success, and it's time to make a change.

Guiding (and intentionally building) the emotional balance of your company isn't an easy task, but in some ways it's the most important work of an organization's leadership. By letting go of the fragile clay pottery, by allowing it to break if it will break, you free your employees to take on projects of greater risk, and deliver greater reward for the company. If you ever hear employees say, "That's an old problem; we'll never fix it," you're hearing the voice of a culture that prefers known failure to unknown success, and it's time to make a change.

THE UNSEEN ELEMENT

Culture, as Henry Ford described it, is the way people are when no one is watching. That can mean the ways they behave, think, talk, work and act. As I've said before, culture is all-encompassing and hugely important — but it's also *unseen*. It's invisible and unwatchable, except in its results. How do you influence something that you can't see, that takes so little form, and yet that is so important?

> How do you influence something that you can't see, that takes so little form, and yet that is so important?

It starts with a good, hard look in the mirror. Corporate culture is, first and foremost, a reflection of the leaders' values, and it's made in the image of the leaders' words and deeds. You have an important role to play in this at all times.

Let me give you an example of a healthy corporate culture: Toyota. Toyota has sustained and advanced their corporate value of waste elimination through a policy of "do things right the first time." Toyota is a good working example of Edward Deming's *quality chain reaction*, which holds that, when quality is the driving force of the culture, it will increase efficiency and productivity, decrease costs and, in turn, allow the company to lower prices, attract a higher market share, increase profits and improve customer satisfaction. Notice that customer satisfaction is directly linked to the actions of employees — even employees on the assembly line thousands of miles away!

You'll notice, too, that the key to this equation isn't scientific or economic mumbo-jumbo; it's people. People are the most important element of a company for achieving customer satisfaction, period.

Talented, well-trained people bring stability to your company. Stability yields trust and accountability, two of the most important traits for a corporate culture, and especially for a culture about to enter an aggressive continuous improvement program.

From your vantage point as a leader and culture-driver, trust and accountability aren't just about knowing that your employees will "do their jobs" without supervision. Trust and accountability are about empowering your employees to do better by themselves, to shoot for better targets of quality. And trust is two-way: Just as you must trust your employees, they must trust you and want to listen. That's why one of your roles is to identify defects blamelessly and then choose technical tools of process improvement to streamline work and eliminate waste. Everyone wins where there's mutual trust and accountability.

Healthy, effective work cultures also display respect for people and intentional human development. If we were in grade school, we'd just call these "respect" and "maturity." And fittingly, because this is just the grown-up, corporate version of the same basic idea. When people respect one another and feel free to do whatever we do best, the office, just as is the case with the schoolyard, is a prosperous place.

Human development is what separates Lean successes from Lean failures. At Toyota, where the level of human development is quite high, employees (a) are in charge of their own jobs, (b) design their own standardized work and (c) are authorized to make changes to improve the work. For any sort of Lean culture to work, you must invest in quality *through your people*, who are the force that build your company and the group ultimately responsible for continuous improvement.

> Human development is what separates
> Lean successes from Lean failures.

Without engaging the hearts of your employees, the results will be marginal (at best).

LEADERS LISTEN WITH PURPOSE

I told you before to look in the mirror. I'll tell you now to look there again, because now we discuss leadership — you — and what the role of a leader is in this task.

Put shortly, it's the role of a leader to create a consistency of purpose toward improving human talent and trust and reducing waste everywhere in the organization. In other words, you have to know that you want people to "tune into" their work as closely as possible, and you have to welcome them to do so *through your example*.

First and most important, you will not accomplish anything unless you *listen with purpose* to the people who perform value-adding work (which, in theory, should be everyone). Think of *the company itself* as a collection of customers and suppliers; everyone in the office has products and services, and among them there is plenty of exchange every day. The same way you want your eventual, external paying customer to be happy and engaged, you want that from your employees (your internal customers), all of whom are consumers of one another's work (and you're a part of that exchange, too).

Secondly, you have to find ways to *show, not tell.* You have to find ways to *show* the change through action, through something that people can witness and remember. If you tell workers that their job is to solve problems, they will forget, or they won't take it to heart; tomorrow they will resume work as before. But if you can *empower* them, if you can show them that their job is to solve problems and that *you trust them* to do it, and that you will help guide them without penalty to them, they will solve problems.

No two companies are the same, of course, but one thing that seems sure is that you won't be doing this from the isolation of your executive office. You'll have to "lead from the shop floor," or whatever your company's equivalent may be. And don't just walk around and ask people how they're doing; engage them, ask them what they need and challenge them to be honest and complete in their answers.

Once you've spent time on the shop floor, the possibilities for improvement will be evident to you. Then, once you've contemplated those possibilities, you'll have a much better idea of how to design structures that will make workers more accountable and more successful.

Weary of Lean Tools?

Leaders are weary of hearing about Lean toolboxes, kanban, standardized work and 5S/6S strategies. These tools, in and of themselves, do not solve problems. All they do, on their own, is increase workload.

This can make problems and problem sources visible, but just adding the steps for one of those programs won't help your company. If you write down goals and add steps, but then permit deviation from those goals and steps, the very tool you bought to improve your company will only showcase the company's weak management or unbelieving leaders. If I may be so blunt, such a leader is not a leader at all; he or she is just a person in charge who is adding pointless steps and diluting the value of the company's work.

> **If you write down goals and add steps, but then permit deviation from those goals and steps, the very tool you bought to improve your company will only showcase the company's weak management or unbelieving leaders.**

One of the leader's jobs is to protect the best interests of the followers — both employees and customers. Happy customers result from happy, engaged employees. Calibrate your corporate culture and they will take care of one another!

Put another way, jobs stay stable when customers are happy. If customers are not happy — perhaps because the company's processes are unstable and the customer is not being consistently served well — jobs are lost. Everyone wants the former; no one wants the latter.

Again, Lean strategies and other tools are not destined to fail or succeed in and of themselves. The difference between their failure and their success is this: they will succeed if they cause people to think about their own work processes. They will succeed if they increase creativity, collaboration and motivation among the employees. They will fail otherwise. Again, this is largely a function of whether you (the leader) respect and invest in the tools; if you don't, they won't.

I'll pause to emphasize collaboration, because it's one of the major catalysts that sustain a continuous improvement culture. Whenever people are able to constructively come together about work, their creativity spikes and their motivation increases — plus, in solving problems, two heads are always better than one. Part of your time and resources for training should focus on collaboration within structure, because it will be an enormous help to everything you're trying to accomplish.

Let me summarize what we've discussed, so you have it all in one place:

> *Lean success is sustained only when leaders and managers develop high trust and problem-solving environments and align incentives to foster an educated and trained workforce that is empowered to work horizontally along the path of workflow. The goal is always to yield a quality employee, who then yields a quality product.*

Hans Christian Andersen wrote a children's short story titled, *The Emperor's New Clothes*. The story illustrates the blinding ambitions of a great emperor who desired to wear the finest silk in the world. Slave to his own desire to possess the best, swindlers fed his foolish ambition, explaining that their silk is so exceptional and magical it appears invisible to any man who was unfit for his office or unpardonably stupid. Silenced by fear, nobody in the kingdom admitted they saw nothing. The emperor's invisible clothes were greatly admired. Finally, a little child, with no fear of criticism, standing or retribution cried, "Good heavens, he has nothing on at all!" That made a deep impression upon the emperor, for it seemed to him that they were right; sadly, he thought to himself, "Now I must bear up to the end."

In a true Lean management culture, you do not have to have all the answers, but you must build a cultural environment that makes it safe for your people to speak truth and resolve conflict. If your Lean launch has grown cold, you must begin by sincerely asking the people why the tools have not lasted, or worked. If your culture and its effects are truly invisible — like the emperor's clothes — it is a reflection of something, and maybe it's time to start again, this time more honestly.

Secret of Change

Are you always working on something? Striving to improve yourself?
Do you frequently experience waves of anxiety, whispering to you
that you aren't working hard enough?

It starts as a small and irritating mood, a little voice reminding you
that you're not eating right, you're not exercising, that all the incomplete projects in the basement sit waiting and unfinished. You question yourself — why haven't you been able to save more money this
year? *Is it already time to clean the garage again? Now work is pushing me to get another physical! My car, wow, it should be way cleaner.
I need more intentional time with my kids. Why do I always feel so
impatient? When was the last time I went on a date night with my
spouse? Did we forget to winterize the lawn mower? Did I really have
to yell at the dog for that?*

If these questions sound all too familiar, you're not alone. Most of us
are tired of trying, in some way, to change our habits or behavior or
attitude for the better. There's an endless supply of self-help materials
on changing bad habits and on improving personal effectiveness;

I knew that like everyone else. But I got lost in the endless litany of arrogant psychologists who babble on and on about wasted "life energy." It all reads like another big gulp of bitter drive-thru guilt. Expensive, boxed, shrink-wrapped, shiny, but guilt-ridden all the same.

But here's the truth ... Guilt is not an effective motivator.

When I realize this, it's because I've thought about the quote above — about building something new rather than focusing on fighting the past or the present. When I think about changing myself, it resonates with me. Generally, I begin to wish for change when something from past choices haunts me in my current situation. This latent pain, when it fully hits someone, jerks them into uncomfortable awareness. And then, let the guilt begin!

Pain can be emotional, physical, or mental — nevertheless, it hurts, and because of that, it can sharpen our sincere desires for change. But is it a good *motivator* for change? Pain usually causes me to start listing everything that brought me to my current unhappy place, and a mountain of negative self-lecture dumps on my head. No one can lecture me more harshly than I lecture myself. I know best what my bad habits look like.

But guilt is a good thing, right? Isn't that why we all make New Year's Resolutions? No. Using negative emotions to spur on self-improvement and self-discipline rarely ends well. How many of you have already given up on a resolution made less than a year ago? *Try and try again, right?* Wrong. This is where negative motivation goes seriously wrong. While guilt is fresh, so is our commitment — but once we get over the moment's pain, we lose our motivation, in the same way that even the blackest bruise only hurts when pressed. When things get tough, we revert to old habits — the standard *modus operandi.*

> While guilt is fresh, so is our commitment — but
> once we get over the moment's pain, we lose
> our motivation, in the same way that even the
> blackest bruise only hurts when pressed.

Old habits die hard. Without fail, we keep thinking about what we *don't* want to be, while trying to start a new journey to become what we *do* want to be. These diverging thoughts don't allow us to release old, bad habits. Habits, after all, help us; subconsciously, we hold onto them, even save them for times of extreme trial. The part of our identity that disappoints us is temporarily hushed, but not removed. Repeatedly focusing on the negative causes us to victimize, to look around for people to blame, even to turn on ourselves and think ugly thoughts. These are mental habits, like any others, and they prevent proactive and positive growth.

I think Millman had it right: focus on building the new in place of the old. Instead of fighting the old you — hating the old habits, loathing the diet, cheating on the budget — figure out what the new you will look like. *What does it truly want? What will it feel like? What will it bring you?* Then, act accordingly. Make choices that are in line with where you are heading. Start small, self-reward and self-encourage. Don't come from the negative perspective of NO and self-deprivation — no chocolate, no spending, no couch potato time. Instead, frame it as YES — yes to nutritious food that stops disease, yes to financial security, yes to more exercise because it's fun, yes to family time because it will mean something for your children.

And, of course, yes to big investments of heart and mind into your continuous improvement culture at work.

How to build better habits that replace the old? This is a secret worth telling.

Do It (Lean) Daily

Operating Lean is a cultural change. It requires change at all levels in all departments of an organization. For that cultural change to occur, you need widespread participation in improvement activities.

Kaizen activities can and should be completed daily. Consider these three huge improvements that were made after brief kaizen meetings:

1. The design of a fixture table used for holding two-by-two-inch square tubing in place as it was welded to create a frame had locating stops and pins that required the welder to manually tighten 10 large C-clamps. A brief kaizen activity resulted in the C-clamps being replaced with toggle clamps. It only took a couple of hours to make the improvement, but the setup time dropped by 60 percent. It was also a great ergonomic improvement.

2. In another example involving a fixture for a medium-sized weldment, a welder was having problems flipping the fixture, as it got heavier with every piece he welded onto the assembly. During a kaizen activity, a co-worker suggested mounting the weldment to an engine stand. One was purchased for $250, and the welder was able to rotate the weldment easily from one side to the other.

3. At a fabricating facility, it was noticed that steel trucks tended to back up in the parking lot as the day went on. Some days, the company was paying several workers overtime to stay and unload trucks that should have been unloaded during the

normally scheduled first shift. A brief discussion with the supervisor and a material handler resulted in an instant analysis of the warehouse.

After watching the trucks being unloaded, the group determined not all of them had to be unloaded via crane; forklifts could unload some. The ones that could be handled by forklift could be unloaded more quickly by using several forklifts at once. An unloading schedule was created that identified each truck as a crane-unload or forklift-unload. Each truck was given a specific time to arrive at the warehouse. When it came time to unload a truck, a minimum of two forklifts were scheduled to be there to unload them. These trucks were generally unloaded in about 15 minutes compared to a truck requiring crane unloading, which averaged 45 minutes. The overtime was eliminated after the kaizen activity.

The chart on the following page is a side-by-side comparison of kaizen activities and kaizen events. It is not meant to be a judgment of which is better; it simply compares the traits and what is necessary to execute the two methodologies in a typical manufacturing environment.

Kaizen activities have a cumulative effect that builds over time into large-scale improvements.

Don't get me wrong. Large-scale kaizen events are sometimes necessary, but generally only when you are making large systematic changes. Kaizen events tend to involve a relatively small group of people, usually subject-matter experts and those with the power to approve changes. Yes, they are normally cross-functional teams, which is good, but they also tend to be heavily laden with engineers and other front-office professionals. Operators may feel a bit intimidated if they are on a team in which the majority of members

KAIZEN ACTIVITY	KAIZEN EVENT
Simple	Complex
Resource Light	Resource Heavy
Short in Duration	Long in Duration
Train As You Go	Trained Prior to Event
Involves Small- and Medium-Sized Groups	Involves Small Groups
Easy-to-Correct Mistakes	Moderate- to Difficult-to-Correct Mistakes
Minimal Preparation Time Required	Extensive Preparation Time Required

aren't their peers. You want them to feel comfortable and to understand that their opinions and suggestions are vital to the success of the kaizen.

Conversely, kaizen *activities* should be led by shop floor operators assisted by their supervisors and managers. Lean is successful only when all people at all levels are actively and continuously leading improvement efforts.

> **Lean is successful only when all people at all levels are actively and continuously leading improvement efforts.**

Who is going to sustain your improvement? Most of the time, it will be the operators on the floor. If the operators are the leaders of kaizen activities, then it is in their best interests to sustain the improvements they have made. If only a minimal number of operators participate in an event, the improvements could very possibly require supervisory and managerial monitoring to ensure they are sustained. Isn't it a much better scenario for supervisors and managers to identify and move forward with the next improvement rather than spend their time monitoring improvements already made?

There is another aspect of kaizen events that many people don't want to talk about, often keeping it in the dark shadows: *What if the kaizen event isn't successful?* Most manufacturing leaders were taught sometime in their careers that they shouldn't plan for failure. This is a solid credo but, at the same time, a manufacturing manager has to have an idea how an unsuccessful kaizen event will affect continuous improvement efforts moving forward.

Obviously, shop floor operators and senior staff watch kaizen events very carefully. They want to see how the new process works, and at the end they offer their judgment: Are changes for the better? If an event was unsuccessful but the company has conducted successful ones previously, then management shouldn't be too concerned because employees understand. However, if a company is just beginning its Lean journey, employees could become more skeptical and immediately doubt the benefits of any Lean Manufacturing exercises.

You want your continuous improvement efforts to build confidence and enthusiasm for continuing the Lean Manufacturing journey. Lost confidence can cross all levels and areas of an organization. For example, if a mechanical engineering manager had to support the kaizen event with one of his or her senior engineers for a week and the event wasn't successful, the manager may be less willing to provide resources and set aside time for the next event. If a company had to schedule overtime to build stock to cover the time diverted to conducting the event, the controller may be less inclined to support future events. Kaizen events tend to be resource-dependent and, as such, if they aren't successful, it may be more challenging to assemble those resources for the next one.

Kaizen activities, on the other hand, are generally simple and short in duration, which also means they require fewer resources. They are also quite often used as teaching opportunities.

For example, the "stand in a circle" technique is a good way to instruct others. You teach them the technique and let them identify improvement opportunities, and then they are released to go and act on those improvement ideas.

If an idea isn't successful, then the teaching opportunity continues. Why didn't the improvement idea work? What could have been done differently? Can a correction be made that could turn the failure into a success? As kaizen activities are less complicated and shorter in duration than kaizen events, a failure associated with an unsuccessful activity won't have the same negative overall impact as a failure linked to a large-scale event.

In the end, both kaizen activities and kaizen events are a necessary part of the fabric of successful manufacturing operations all over the world. Most organizations will conduct a combination of the two. Both have their advantages and disadvantages. It's just a question of which combination of the two will most quickly and successfully move the company forward in establishing a culture of continuous improvement.

HARMONY IS POWERFUL JAM: A FINAL WORD ON EXECUTIVE LEADERSHIP

Throughout this book, we have focused on the ways in which continuous improvement cultures are created and nurtured — up, down and across organizations. I have endeavored to remind you, at every turn, that your success requires every employee. Sense everything that is possible in your organization often starts as a conversation in a boardroom, I'd be remiss not to offer some insights on how to make those boardroom conversations more productive and harmonious. So, before concluding this book — which has been a distinct honor to write for you, and which I hope has provided you with some nuggets of inspiration — I'd like to offer a final word on executive leadership, specifically on how leaders can brainstorm more effectively.

Bear with me as I serve up a final analogy, this time about music. A musical "jam session," by its own definition, is an organized mess, unscripted. It starts somewhere and ends somewhere else. Songs find a groove and a beat, and invite their makers to improvise from point "a" to point "b," with as much deviation and derivation as talent allows. Players must always honor the purpose to remain in harmony, but other than that, everyone is *an individual* and *valued contributor.*

Jazz is a series of great jam sessions, all returning to a familiar harmony. The better the players, the greater the distance between melody and improvisation, between established rhythms and off-beats, and the more likely it is that the music rises to that magical in-between space that we call art. John Coltrane's version of "My Favorite Things" is a distinct example of how far an artist can travel from the familiar, visit something completely new and never really leave home.

Band members decide on a series of musical journeys they want to take during a concert and then set out to take them, *together*.

Why can't business executives find that sweet harmonious spot of mutually contributing thoughts and ideas? How do you get a room full of stressed-out, competitive executives to harmonize, together?

I suggest you jam.

In all Jam Sessions, certain principles override:

- It is genius to listen to others while playing your own instrument.

- The joy of achieving a unity, somehow and somewhere during the jam.

- A superior ability to improvise and interpret, on the spot, without much to rely on but instinct.

- A grasp of the technical skills.

All of these concepts work exceptionally well in music, but they can also work in business settings, where an executive is trying to get the most from the team. It is all about perspective; when successful leaders inspire each other, and choose not to compete with one another, but to *complete* one another, there is harmony ... art.

Complex problems demand sophisticated and complex solutions rarely developed by a single input, but by a team of thinkers working toward a common result. The whole group, listening to each other and working together to solve the problem, can face issues that need discussion. If the forum created allows and encourages innovative thinking, creativity will flood in and find its rightful place in the room, bringing with it crisp new ideas and possibilities.

Here are some questions to ask before a Jam Session meeting begins:

1. **What Song Are We Playing (PURPOSE)?**
    Clearly identify the point of the meeting, its purpose and place, and what types of solutions are being sought. Agree on a purpose; be certain of what you are going after and what you want the room to chase. Everyone needs to know the tune (purpose).

2. **Who Wants to Be the Big Dog (WHO WILL RISK AND MODEL)?**
    Who will the first player to show his or her skills and acumens to the rest of the room? The player best suited to this task should always handle the first presentation. This will change depending upon the song and the day and everyone should know that who-ever it is, it takes a lot of courage to be first. The team should be looking forward to listening to what he or she is presenting. This individual will step up and set the bar for the rest of the team, being the first to come forward with good ideas, solvable prob-lems, workable innovations and interesting solutions.

3. **How Much Time Do We Get (FACILITATORS GUARD TEMPO)?**
    Everyone involved in the meeting should take as much or as little time as they want to take. A good jam establishes its own pace and operates most successfully without clear lines or boundar-ies. Everyone with an instrument/idea has a right to take enough time to play and get ideas conceived, performed, explored and finalized. Time is a friend, not an enemy. Tempo is a guideline,

not a restriction. Other jam thinkers are partners, not competitors. The room is full of teammates who can take the essence of any idea and turn it a different direction.

4. **Anyone Up for Trading Fours (BRAINSTORMING)?**
   One of the other best moments in a good jam is when the players "trade" ideas. Usually this is counted in measures, or bars. Four bars for one player, then four for another, then back again and back again, until that particular idea is exhausted. This is a great technique for the conference room, where two individuals are back and forth with each other in a quick exchange of exploration and innovation of a particular stream of consciousness. The bandleader takes the jam there and so should the executive. Want to change it up and keep the meeting alive and well? Start trading ideas.

5. **Did You Hear That (REALLY LISTEN)?**
   Listening to what the other participants come up with in a jam session can be the most important contribution to what any other individual may create. One person's idea is the inspiration for everyone else's detail. There are no completely new ideas, so it is in the subtleties that the harmony is found, and the only way to be sure to hear them is to listen. Humans are most creative when we LISTEN.

A good jam session brings out the best and the brilliance in all participants. It will bring out the same in the executives sitting in the conference room trying to identify great ideas for your company to use going forward. When the desire for harmony is valued more than individual performance, a powerful jam session begins.

Putting it All Together

As shared throughout this book, our intent was twofold:

1. To provide a simple proven path to changing and sustaining the culture of your business with specific examples of methods, rationale and results.

2. To provide tools and ideation to be used for the actual implementation of the change, ongoing maintenance and continued operation of the system.

A few words of caution: The CI Helix cannot be used for a partial implementation just to produce rapid results. Many managers have tried to implement "rules" to change behavior to drive actions or improve results. Without first evaluating and establishing organizational values, intentionally creating value aligned experiences, and nurturing the desired changes to behavior and actions, results will not sustain. Behavior, action and results are built upon and sustained through a top-down commitment to clearly defined and embraced values.

A note of encouragement and hope: This system, when combined with a true gain-sharing program, can provide amazing results in productivity and profitability.

5 REASONS WHY PEOPLE RESIST CHANGE

Have heart. Your decision to create and nurture a CI culture is a wise one. But it won't always be easy, and people won't always jump on board right away. Remember that resistance to change is a natural phenomenon, and keep in mind why people resist. Understanding their reactions will help you to help them through it so that, someday soon, everyone in your company is as confident and committed as you are in this moment. You've got this!

There are perhaps five main reasons why people resist change, even when that change is overwhelmingly promising:

1. **Fear of the Unknown/Surprise:** This type of resistance occurs mainly when change is implemented without warning the affected stakeholders before the change occurs. When change (especially what is perceived as difficult change) is pushed onto people without giving them adequate warning and without helping them through the process of understanding what the change will include and how their jobs/work will be affected, it can cause people to push back against the change due to their fear of the unknown.

2. **Mistrust:** If the individuals in a department highly respect their manager because the manager has built up trust over time, the team will be more accepting of any changes. If the manager is new and has not yet earned the trust of their employees, then mistrust can manifest itself into resistance to change.

3. **Loss of Job Security/Control:** This type of resistance often occurs when companies announce they will be restructuring

(downsizing is the received message). This causes fear among employees that they will lose their jobs or be moved into other positions without their input.

4. **Bad Timing:** As the old saying goes, "Timing is everything." Too much change on employees over a short period of time can cause resistance. If change is not implemented at the right time or with the right level of tact or empathy, it usually won't work.

5. **An Individual's Predisposition Toward Change:** Differences exist in people's overall tolerance for change. Some people enjoy change because it provides them with an opportunity to learn new things and grow personally and professionally. Others fear change because they prefer a set routine — these are usually the people who become suspicious of change and are more likely to resist.

The bottom line is this — Whether you're the CEO, a department manager or your company's CI specialist, you will frequently find yourself in the role of "change agent." And it's the change agent's responsibility to understand …

1. WHAT the specific changes include.

2. WHO the changes will impact.

3. HOW it will impact those people.

4. WHY they might resist the changes.

When you know those things and approach the changes — and the people — with compassion and in alignment with the organization's values, you're headed for success.

If you continually embrace the management-engaged audit process and relentlessly seek improvement of your own continuous improvement system, it will serve you well indefinitely. As suggested herein, give your culture a name and identified logo; it will become the crown jewel of your business and will be affectionately referred to by all team members, as it represents both success and reward. And that is the essence of culture.

GREAT LEADERS, KIND READERS - YOU

> "But those who hope in the Lord will renew their strength. They will soar on wings like eagles; they will run and not grow weary, they will walk and not be faint."
>
> — *Isaiah 40:31, New International Version*

Good leaders must persevere through the tiresome work of enforcing discipline every day. Too many times, we start an initiative (the flavor of the day) only to turn it over to someone else to sustain. Building a sustainable culture requires the shepherd to constantly encourage, evaluate and seek improvement. If you do not already know, being the shepherd of any team will require you to be lonely, brave, sacrificial and encouraging to others when you don't have anything left to give. It requires that you refuse to *grow faint in the face of adversity.*

It is our hope and prayer that the humorous stories and serious Lean strategies in this book may help at least one young leader to recognize that your business is leaving gold in the fields of manufacturing if your employees do not really trust and believe in your vision. Our two parting phrases of encouragement are ... *It's all about the leader and people watch what the boss watches.* Demonstrate leadership — live it every day by protecting your team members in both word and deed. Next, discipline your own eyes to focus on actions that add value. Stop talking about it and start building your culture of continuous improvement; the team will follow your lead. *"Shut Up and Get Lean."*

EPILOGUE

What comes after this book? Inspiring work for you and your colleagues!

But what comes after Lean? I've been perplexed by this question. I can't imagine an end to "doing CI Lean." Lean remains, in many ways, an inexhaustible strategy. On the other hand, I haven't come across any new methodologies for sustaining continuous improvement.

Frederick Winslow Taylor's Big Idea of 1883, to separate brains from hands, is further advanced by today's intuitive Big Data processors. Every day, human craftsmanship is being coded and translated into algorithms, which are freeing both human brain and hand. Couple Big Idea Management with Big Data Solutions and you get a world seated at the feet of ... Amazon.

As much as I am a fan of Amazon, here is a case where the shopkeeper has been replaced by an automated web interface that has already analyzed your search and purchase history, and anticipated your future purchase. Humans follow the instructions dictated by these prodigy systems, pick and pack the item, and deliver it to your front door. All this accomplished and you never had to take off your house slippers. That's innovation, right?

This brave new world of Big Idea and Big Data commerce is clearly going to continue. Taylor would have never imagined how his desire to establish a "best and efficient method" could have evolved into an age of algorithms predicting how humans would spend hard-earned dollars on Black Friday. But here we are.

Maybe I am having a difficult time adjusting to our hyper techno-logically obsessed world. Am I the only person to find it ridiculous to order a Starbucks coffee from a cell phone app minutes before arriving to pick it up? Would someone else just drink it for me? In our urgency to do things with greater efficiency, have we gone too far with the intentional separation of the human intellect (brains) from problem solving (working hands)? This all feels a little Orwellian.

One strong movement that I find incredibly timely (and it is all about saving time) is Design Thinking. It partners well with Lean Thinking and gives hope that we will not become slave to Big Data while our brains atrophy. Design Thinking can be traced back to two primary sources: Herbert A. Simon's 1969 book, *The Sciences of the Artificial*, and Robert McKim's 1972 design engineering book, *Experiences in Visual Thinking*.

Design Thinking presents a formal method for practical problem solving; however, its approach differs from the analytical *scientific method*, which begins by thoroughly defining all parameters of a problem to create a solution (problem-focused). Design Thinking identifies and investigates both known and unclear (ambiguous) pieces of the current situation to discover alternative paths that may lead to a desired solution (solution-focused).

Scientists problem-solve by analysis, and designers problem-solve by synthesis. Design Thinking engages both analysis and synthesis. Unlike analytical thinking alone (Big Data), Design Thinking includes gathering or stealing ideas, with no limits on brainstorming. (By the way, algorithms can't brainstorm.) Open brainstorming reduces fear of failure among participants and encourages participation from a wide variety of sources in the ideation phase. *Thinking outside the box* describes one strategy of Design Thinking, as it aids in the discovery of uncharted solutions and challenges faulty assumptions long imbedded in organizational cultures. (Computers can't challenge culture; it is illogical.)

Whereas Lean Thinkers believe that human creativity needs to be put back into the system at the operations kaizen level, Design Thinkers argue *that businesspeople need to be skilled at design to creatively invent the products and services of tomorrow.* This is not incompatible with Lean; it's complementary. The economies of scale that were the hallmark of the 20th century are now less significant than our imagination to produce elegant, refined and targeted solutions for our customers. "Imagination" is replacing "scale," and if you doubt this, do some research on the number of iPhones released in the past three years. If you still doubt the impact of imagination on economics, pick up a biography of Walt Disney.

1. The first assumption of Design Thinking is that innovation touches everything that surrounds us: objects certainly, but also economies, cultures and political systems.

2. Second is that great design can be taught (and learned) through a better understanding of key design problem solving, as opposed to algorithms in static IT systems.

3. Design Thinking is all about creating variation, and variation is all about providing innovative solutions.

Lean Thinking has traditionally focused on making legacy systems work; Design Thinking seeks to free thinkers from legacy systems. Both strategies are exciting, and although fundamentally different (one kaizen-driven, the other innovation driven), both place the human being at the center of the business process. "Great people make great products" is a central assumption common to both fields. Individual life experience, paradigms, and the available creativity and engagement a person brings to their job ... these things cannot be procedural and built into any rule-based-system. They change and evolve, they grow, or they die.

> **Lean Thinking has traditionally focused on making legacy systems work; Design Thinking seeks to free thinkers from legacy systems.**

Lean's core question, "How do we develop people to design better products?" is more relevant than ever. Perhaps Design Thinking asks, "How do we design organizational cultures that develop better thinkers?"

No matter what the future holds, no matter how Lean Thinking is impacted by Design Thinking or how different Lean tools are refined and revolutionized in the future, business leaders will always need the basics lessons and imperatives to create and sustain culture as presented herein. I remain impassioned about what is possible when organizations commit to continuous improvement because I have seen, first hand, what it makes possible — the careers, the satisfied customers, the bottom-line results.

MENTAL NOTE

Design Thinking is the "SPICE" ingredient that scientific- and physics (engineering)-driven companies forget, even disregard. There is no innovation, no stepping in front of the future, unless someone in the organization is thinking "beyond" outside-of-the-box.

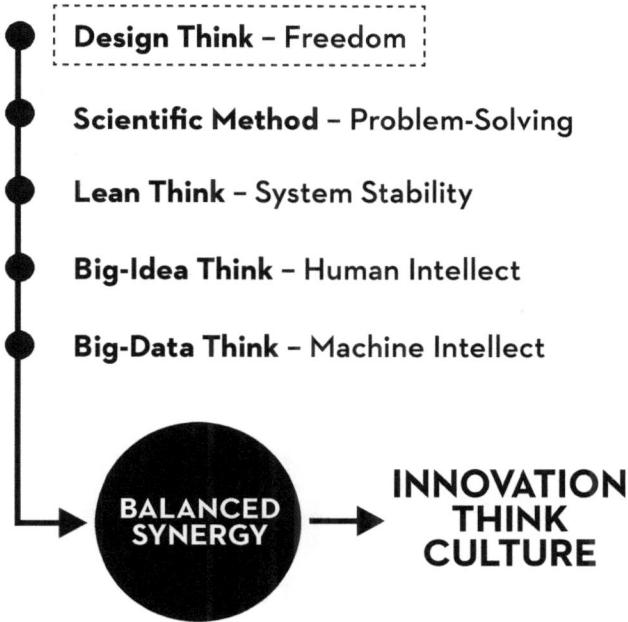

CI Helix

When I set out to write this book, I kept imagining the CI Helix graphic that was introduced in Chapter 6. A helix is a curved line that appears to move upward, like an infinite staircase. The double helix is two such lines opposite one another, twisting together, and that's the shape of our most important, most intelligent molecule: DNA. DNA is the complete set of instructions that guide the development and function of all known living beings. In my mind, there is no more appropriate image than the double helix for visualizing Continuous Improvement Culture: progressive, connected, intertwined elements that build upwards upon one another and provide structure for a successful, sustainable business.

To capture material to build this book, we created a website: CIhelix.com. We encourage you to download anything you find useful from the site, and to visit often to find new resources and tools.

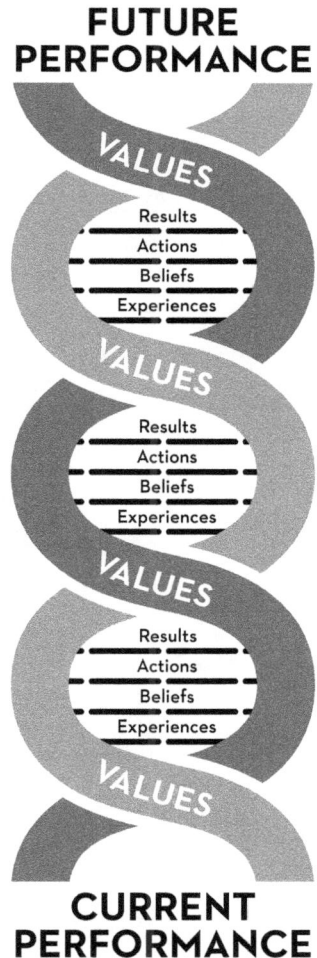

FUTURE PERFORMANCE

VALUES

Results
Actions
Beliefs
Experiences

VALUES

Results
Actions
Beliefs
Experiences

VALUES

Results
Actions
Beliefs
Experiences

VALUES

CURRENT PERFORMANCE

The CI Helix, ©2019, Ray Leathers

Because I like to motivate others to action, and enjoy being emotionally motivated, I have littered this text with some original and some borrowed quotes that my colleagues and I deem valuable. I hope you use these to inspire your own journey, and I thank you for taking this journey of reading and learning with me. I appreciate your time and your trust. Before you go, be sure to check out the Keep in Touch page at the end of the book. I look forward to seeing you on social media, at an industry event, or one-on-one. I hope this is just the beginning.

REFERENCES

Captain D. Michael Abrashoff, *It's Your Ship: Management Techniques from the Best Damn Ship in the Navy,* Grand Central Publishing, 2012 (Revised and updated edition).

Summer Allen, "The Science of Generosity," White Paper for the John Templeton Foundation, Greater Good Science Center, University of California at Berkeley, May 2018.

Hans Christian Andersen, *The Emperor's New Clothes,* C.A. Reitzel, 1837.

John Coltrane, *My Favorite Things* Album, Atlantic Records, 1961.

Roger Connors and Tom Smith, *Change the Culture, Change the Game: The Breakthrough Strategy for Energizing Your Organization and Creating Accountability for Results,* Penguin Group, 2011.

Roger Connors, Tom Smith and Craig Hickman, *The Oz Principle: Getting Results Through Individual and Organizational Accountability,* Portfolio, 2010 (Revised and updated edition).

Stephen Covey, *7 Habits of Highly Effective People: Powerful Lessons in Personal Change,* Free Press, 1989.

Todd Herman, "Personal Accountability," *Todd Herman Associates,* 2000-2009.

Catherine Ryan Hyde, *Pay It Forward,* Simon & Schuster, 1999.

Robert H. McKim, *Experiences in Visual Thinking*, Brooks/Cole Publishing, 1972.

Menander, *Dyskolos*, 317 B.C.

Dan Millman, *Way of the Peaceful Warrior: A Book That Changes Lives*, 2006 (Revised edition).

Mirriam-Webster, *Mirriam-Webster's Dictionary and Thesarus*, 2014 (Revised and updated edition).

Oxford Dictionaries, *Concise Oxford English Dictionary*, Oxford University Press, 2011.

Phil Alden Robinson, *Field of Dreams* Movie, Universal Pictures, 1989.

Shigeo Shingo, *A Revolution in Manufacturing: The SMED System*, Productivity Press, 1985.

Herbert A. Simon, *The Sciences of the Artificial*, M.I.T. Press, 1969.

U.S. Bureau of Labor Statistics, "Workplace Injuries," *National Safety Council*, 2018.

Cy Wakeman, "Personal Accountability and The Pursuit of Workplace Happiness," *Forbes,* Oct. 26, 2015.

Additional Recommended Reading

What follows is a select list of books I have found beneficial in building and maintaining a culture of continuous improvement and, therefore, books you might enjoy. For an ever-green list of recommended books, visit www.CIhelix.com to see my latest thoughts.

- *Change the Culture, Change the Game: The Breakthrough Strategy for Energizing Your Organization and Creating Accountability for Results*, Roger Connors and Tom Smith

- *The Go-Giver: A Little Story About a Powerful Business Idea*, Bob Burg and John David Mann

- *Who Moved My Cheese?: An A-Mazing Way to Deal with Change in Your Work and in Your Life*, Spencer Johnson, MD

- *It's Your Ship: Management Techniques from the Best Damn Ship in the Navy*, Captain D. Michael Abrashoff

- *QBQ! The Question Behind the Question: Practicing Personal Accountability at Work and in Life*, John G. Miller

- *Coach to the Goal: Ten Truths to Turn Your Team into Winners,* Michael Duke

MORE TITLES TO CONSIDER

- *Creating a Lean Culture: Tools to Sustain Lean Conversions,* David Mann

- *Mary Kay Way: Timeless Principles from America's Greatest Woman Entrepreneur,* Mary Kay Ash

- *The Five Dysfunctions of a Team: A Leadership Fable,* Patrick Lencioni

- Any *"Leadership"* book by John Maxwell

- *The Speed of Trust: The One Thing That Changes Everything,* Stephen M.R. Covey

- *It Isn't Just Business, It's Personal: How PAETEC Thrived When All the Big Telecoms Couldn't,* Arunas A. Chesonis and David Dorsey

- *Mojo: How to Get It, How to Keep It, How to Get It Back If You Lose It,* Marshall Goldsmith

- *How to Become a Great Boss: The Rules for Getting and Keeping the Best Employees,* Jeffrey J. Fox

- *The Shack: Where Tragedy Confronts Eternity* (for spiritual motivation), William Paul Young

- *The Leadership Pipeline: How to Build the Leadership Powered Company,* Ram Charan

- *The Four Disciplines of Execution: Achieving Your Wildly Important Goals,* Chris McChesney, Sean Covey and Jim Huling

- *The Oz Principle: Getting Results Through Individual and Organizational Accountability,* Roger Connors, Tom Smith and Craig Hickman

- *Lean for Dummies,* Natalie J. Sayer and Bruce Williams

- *The Race,* Eliyahu M. Goldratt and Robert Fox

- *Team Barriers: Actions for Overcoming the Blocks to Empowerment, Involvement, and High Performance,* Ann and Bob Harper

- *First, Break All the Rules: What the World's Greatest Managers Do Differently,* Marcus Buckingham and Curt Coffman

- *Toyota Production System: Beyond Large-Scale Production,* Taiichi Ohno

- *The One Minute Manager* (Or the revised edition *New One Minute Manager*), Kenneth Blanchard, PhD and Spencer Johnson, MD

- *The Soul of Leadership: Unlocking Your Potential for Greatness,* Deepak Chopra, M.D.

- *Servant Leadership: A Journey into the Nature of Legitimate Power and Greatness,* Robert K. Greenleaf

- *Help the Helper: Building a Culture of Extreme Teamwork,* Kevin Pritchard and John Eliot

- *The Charge: Activating the Ten Human Drives That Make You Feel Alive,* Brendon Burchard

- *Adapt: Why Success Always Starts with Failure,* Tim Harford

- *The Modern Theory of the Toyota Production System: A Systems Inquiry of the World's Most Emulated and Profitable Management System,* Phillip Marksberry, PhD, PE

Acknowledgments

We are simple people and have attempted to address a complex subject: organizational culture. In this modest book, these acknowledgments are from our hearts. It is our hope to convey our gratitude for those who have bent, shaped and refined the persons we are grateful to be today, and to acknowledge those who have made this book possible.

FAITH

As servants of faith, we begin all things by recognizing and thanking God, who has been a perfect Father and our constant friend.

BOOK COACH AND PUBLISHING TEAM

One of the more recent influences that we acknowledge is our publishing team. As with most first-time authors, we didn't know we had a book in us. If you have lived the subject, know you have a book to write, but are not sure you can dig it out of the busy chapters of your life, these are the treasure hunters who can map it into your story. They are unpretentious supporters, coaches and experts, who make daunting challenges attainable. If you've ever thought about writing a book, reach out to Cathy Fyock, the book coach who helped us turn an idea into a manuscript, then call Kate Colbert at Silver Tree

Publishing to make your manuscript stronger, your book more beautiful and your approach to the marketplace more meaningful.

A huge note of thanks goes to our early readers and endorsers, who took the time to review this book prior to publication, to share their encouraging words and to support us in this undertaking.

VOESTALPINE

We especially want to thank the management of voestalpine of Linz, Austria, corporate owners of Roll Forming Corporation, where Ray served as VP of Operations for seven years and President/CEO for 10 years, and where Susan has served as CIP Lean Specialist for 14 years. After RFC was acquired by voestalpine in 2000, it was apparent that a "turnaround" would be required to survive. voestalpine management afforded us the opportunity to execute the turnaround with total autonomy, a level of trust not commonly demonstrated by new international owners. This is where the concept and value of culture became paramount in our management values. The experiences, many of which are presented in this book, summarize the success that can be obtained through commitment to and sustained implementation of a culture of continuous improvement.

Special Acknowledgements from Ray

FAMILY AND FRIENDS

These acknowledgments must begin with the recognition of the work ethic imparted to me by my family while growing up on tobacco-quilted land in central Kentucky. I didn't realize it at the time, but I was put in the driver's seat of a "work-based learning" experience. I was part owner, leader, manager and laborer in the fields of my family land. These life-sharpening experiences went on to serve me during my studies at Eastern Kentucky University, and continued into my years of military service, and certainly impacted my leadership in numerous manufacturing operations.

To my daughter Melanie, affectionately known as Melo, you are my pride and joy. Born in Germany, during our overseas tour, you were dragged all over the continent. Despite my strongest efforts to the contrary, you have developed into a beautiful, successful woman who makes me proud to be called your "daddy" every day.

I lost my father, "Sonny," more than 26 years ago, and he still crosses my thoughts every day. He was my mentor, my confidante and, most importantly, my best friend. His gentle nature taught me the great investment of treating people with dignity and respect. Someday when I join him in eternity, I will thank him for the unspoken emotional intelligence he imparted to me. Annette, my loving mother, made sure throughout my childhood that I enjoyed the best country breakfast served in Kentucky. I learned servant-hearted service from her every day of my life. If there is anything good in me, it comes from my parents.

Steve Meador, you are my business hero and the best hunting partner an old guy like me could ever wish for. You continue to amaze me with your business wizardry. Dave Wilkins, you have been mentor, life guide and wise counsel in many times of need. Thank you for being a loyal friend and wearing our great country's uniform with me.

EMPLOYERS, MENTORS AND GUIDES

After laboring for years in the Bluegrass fields of Kentucky, lonely and harsh military operations and finally manufacturing arenas, I have discovered, that training is the most important thing we do, but it's the worst thing we do. Other than my Uncle's boot camp on the homestead, the U.S. Military is the most effective training organization I've ever experienced. After all, the Army only does two things: train and fight. And training matters, everywhere.

One of the many things I've learned in my role as commissioner of workforce innovation in the commonwealth of Kentucky is that there is a surprising and disappointing lack of engagement by employers. Business sets on a three-legged stool: (1) capital to fund the business, (2) technology for competitive processes and (3) development of the workforce. Few business leaders embrace the third leg, workforce. Most employers will not invest in the expense of training, the single resource that employs the other two, capital and technology. When I presented the training at Roll Forming Corporation, I was invariably asked how I could afford that much training. My answer: "How can you afford *not* to?" It's the cheapest single investment you can make.

I am grateful to have been trained by amazing people and organizations throughout my career. Across the years, my employers provided various flavors of both practical leadership and Lean strategic applications. Employers who endured and inspired me include: the U.S. Army, Morton Thiokol, Kilgore Companies, Unisys, Southern Scrap Company, Katayama American, voestalpine Roll Forming Corporation and most recently the Commonwealth of Kentucky, where I've been provided the opportunity to improve workforce development for the commonwealth in my role as commissioner of workforce innovation. My mother used to say I couldn't keep a job. The truth is, I kept several amazing ones along the way!

Each of these enterprises added tools to my cache of capabilities. Other than the importance of training discussed above, the Army taught me leadership and provided the opportunity, repeatedly, for practical application in a variety of environments. I was a snotty-nosed 21-year-old green second lieutenant in charge of between 20 and 40 subordinates, some 10 to 20 years my senior. This is where you learn how to earn respect the hard way, which is "doing something for someone no one else can do!" This can be especially traumatic and effective simultaneously if you find yourself in a life-threatening situation, like combat.

Morton Thiokol (Louisiana Army Ammunition Plant) afforded me my first civilian management position as a maintenance superintendent. Once again, I found myself supervising vocational experts 20 to 30 years my senior. Morton management provided the essential support, training, autonomy and reinforcing guidance on managing a 200-man unionized maintenance staff, a 15,000-acre facility with more than 700 buildings, 500 miles of roads and a 100-car railroad. Kilgore, Unisys and Southern Scrap provided similar experiences, most importantly guiding me in the development of my appreciation and value for people, the most important resource of any enterprise. Katayama, a "traditional" privately owned Japanese automotive supplier, taught me the basics of highly disciplined Deming standardization and Lean Manufacturing. Many of these Japanese tools are presented in this book.

CONTRIBUTOR, ADVISOR AND FRIEND

The journey I undertook, resulting in the concepts delivered in this book, would not have been possible without contributions from my business colleague and Lean Manager of 17 years, Susan Nally. Much of the creative ideation for the tools provided herein came from her paradigm and application of the Toyota Production System strategies at voestalpine RFC. Most importantly, she provided the relentless perseverance necessary to realize the long-term benefits of the continuous improvement concepts implemented at RFC. I will always be thankful to Susan for her unflagging dedication — for the times she pressed for the improvement of our team structures and communication systems. She would coax me out of my office, onto the production floor, to see the "magic" unfold during countless employee kaizen efforts. These experiences newly inspired me to focus on what was most important for the internal and external customer, to add value, *to do something the customer is willing to pay for*, in all that we do.

Constructing a culture of continuous improvement is nearly impossible to do while running a business; however, I can promise you that your business will find its early demise if you don't at least try. Hire someone whose job it is to inspire and cheer your leadership to challenge things that are *just good enough.* I hope each of you have such a combat multiplier partner in your corner, one who ceaselessly pushes behind the scenes until organizational vision becomes reality.

About the Authors

RAY LEATHERS

Ray Leathers is a renowned manufacturing industry leader and continuous improvement expert who built his 40-year civilian leadership career upon 18 years of decorated military service in the U.S. Army.

Ray grew up on tobacco farms in the bluegrass lands of Kentucky before heading off to Eastern Kentucky University on a ROTC scholarship. He later earned a master's degree from the University of Southern California. During nearly 18 years of military service (active, guard and reserves), he became a highly decorated officer in the U.S. Army, where he held two commands and was awarded the Army Achievement Medal, two Army Commendation Medals and the Army Meritorious Service Medal. Ray and his family spent four years in Europe during his active duty tour of service.

Ray is a leader with broad global perspectives. His 40-year career in manufacturing included experience in Canada, Japan, Europe, the Caribbean and the United States, and he has worked for American, British, Japanese and Austrian firms.

In 2000, Ray joined Roll Forming Corporation (RFC), the very same year that it was acquired by voestalpine, a leading technology and capital goods group with 500 companies in 50 countries. Ray contributed significantly to RFC's success as part of the senior management team from the very beginning of the company's journey from a family-owned business to a corporate-owned enterprise. In the Japanese environment, Ray learned first-hand the kaizen tool set and other Japanese management methods that, together with the technical advances from European sister divisions, helped him implement the highly successful RFC Continuous Improvement program, which led to yearly cost savings and improved productivity.

In 2007, Ray became the President/CEO of Roll Forming Corporation, leading the organization until his retirement in 2017. Following his retirement from the manufacturing industry, Ray was appointed Commissioner of the Kentucky Department of Workforce Investment.

Ray has long been recognized by professional associations throughout the United States as an innovative leader for the implementation of a Lean culture. He was awarded the 2010 Manufacturing Employee of the Year by the Kentucky Association of Manufacturing, and was presented the Shelby County Distinguished Citizen Award by the Boy Scouts of America.

Ray attributes his passion for community service to his formative days as a Boy Scout in a troop sponsored by his church, where he earned the God and Country Award. Ray is a passionate outdoorsman who enjoys "farming for wildlife" and takes great pride in introducing local youth to what he considers one of our country's greatest freedoms: hunting.

He is a huge promoter of the Shelbyville Community and has held positions on the executive boards for the Shelby County Chamber of Commerce, Shelby County Associated Industries, the Dorman Preschool Center, the Serenity Center, the Shelby County Industrial Development Foundation and numerous other committees focused on the economic development and quality of life of his local community.

SUSAN A. NALLY

Susan A. Nally grew up in Louisville, Kentucky, with her head under the hood of a car, and her two older brothers and dad explaining the physics behind combustion engines in the tiny family garage. Her father was a patent quality engineer for The Ford Motor Co. and her mother was a homemaker and insurance underwriter. Susan attended the University of Louisville for her BA and the University of Kentucky for Lean Certification.

She began her affection for the Nihonjin (Japanese) culture at 12 years of age, when she joined a traditional Yoseikan Karate dojo. Susan trained in martial arts for 14 years, earning a Shodan black belt title at age 21. Lean Production Systems and tools, like the Japanese dojo culture, are rich in discipline, process repetition, preparedness training and respect for the individual. Lean cultures prepare one to tackle daily challenges, so when the unexpected crisis ensues, experience, creativity and hope endure.

Susan began her professional working career with an internship at the British Broadcasting Company in 1988, transitioned into the corporate marketplace as a marketing research specialist with a Louisville-based restaurant chain, Chi-Chi's Corporate, and later joined the JB Speed Art Museum in Louisville, Kentucky. In 1998, she joined RFC as a Lean Specialist and technical writer. While on sabbatical from RFC to achieve her greatest title, mother, she incorporated her part-time consulting business, Lean*Forward* Inc., speaking and training on Lean System strategies, conducting Lean Boot Camps, VSMs, 6S Launches, Team Building Camps and process improvement kaizen events. Today, Susan has returned to her RFC family and is currently serving voestalpine as full-time RFC CIP Lean Manager. Over the years, Susan has served the Shelby County Chamber of Commerce, Wayside Christian Mission, the Dorman Children's Center and Hosparus Health of Louisville. She served on the board of directors at the Shelby County Community Theatre and Operation Care, and is a staff writer for *ShelbyLife Magazine*.

Susan resides in Shelbyville, Kentucky, and is the proud mom of her beloved, adventuresome son, Elijah, and her beautiful and talented daughter, Olivia. Her inspiration and grace come from Him — Romans 8:11.

www.ingramcontent.com/pod-product-compliance
Lightning Source LLC
Chambersburg PA
CBHW071727200326
41519CB00021BC/6605